# FACT or fiction?

## The truth behind urban myths!

**WAYLAND**
www.waylandbooks.co.uk

# Read this bit first...!

Long ago, if something newsworthy happened the only way that the world found out was if someone witnessed the event and told someone else. That someone would tell someone else about it. And so on. The only problem was that the story might change a bit as it was passed on — and so an urban myth was created...

## For example: Giant alligators lurk in New York's sewers!

The arrival of the internet gave urban myths and legends a new lease of life. Things people would never believe by word of mouth take on the ring of truth once they appear on screen. The web has also been responsible for the spread of another kind of urban myth: the incredible-but-apparently-true story...

Here's a quick quiz. Using your skill and judgement (and not the internet), try to guess which of the following bizarre statements are true or false:

- You can get sucked into an aeroplane loo!
- Eating apple pips can poison you!
- Cleopatra, the queen of Egypt, had a beard!
- Mount Everest is getting bigger!
- Weeing on a jellyfish sting will cure it!
- Goldfish have a 3-second memory!

Here's a shocker. They might all sound bonkers, but three of the above are 100% true. But you're going to have to read the book to find out which ones they are!

Prepare to be stunned and amazed as the things you always believed to be true are blown out of the water. Can eating apple pips poison you? Do head lice really prefer clean hair? And do you really swallow spiders in your sleep?

As well as the fact or fiction behind urban myths, discover the deadliest jobs in history and the inventions they thought would never work. Famous words they never said? Check. Ye olde celebrity gossip? That's here too. And much, much more...

So can you disentangle fact from fiction? Read on!

Some people love animals so much, they'll do almost anything to spend time with them. They'll let their dog sleep on the bed, spend a fortune on expensive cat food, or take their pet lobster with them when they go for a walk (see page 40).

There are even a few people who will take their pet snake along to a robbery...

## Case 1: the BMX bandit

A teenager was spotted trying to steal a torch from a hardware store in California, USA. When the staff tried to stop him, he revealed the snake wrapped around his arm. Everyone jumped backwards, and the pesky young thief pedalled off on his bike.

## Case 2: snake not-so-charming

In the Indian capital Delhi, tourists enjoy watching snake charmers. What they're not so keen on is being robbed at snakepoint. Snakes have been used in several crimes in the city. One of the most frightening was when two men coiled a constrictor around a businessman's neck. They refused to remove it until he gave them money.

# USED IN STICK-UPS

## Case 3: the snake stick-up

Two people were walking along the streets of New Jersey, USA one evening when a car screeched to a stop beside them. A man leapt out and brandished a snake, while two more men got out of the car and went through the walkers' pockets.

⭐ **And the truth is...**

These are all real cases — and there have been plenty of others, too. Using a snake as a deadly weapon seems to be on the increase!

Verdict : _____ **FACT** _____

OTHER (TRUE) STORIES ABOUT SNAKES:
1. Dead rattlesnakes can still bite you a day later!

2. Black mambas are not black. They're grey, brown or olive coloured.

3. Seven of the 10 deadliest types of snake live in Australia.

4. Snakes are sometimes born with two heads. The heads of a two-headed snake will fight each other for food, even though they share the same stomach.

## The Titanic was unsinkable!

Well, that's what everyone thought before 15 April 1912.

## ⭐ And the truth is...

*Titanic* hit an iceberg on her maiden voyage between Southampton and New York City and plummeted to the bottom of the Atlantic Ocean. Of the 2,223 people on board, a staggering 1,517 died. This was mostly because of the bone-chilling seawater, which could kill a swimmer in fifteen minutes flat, but also because there weren't enough lifeboats. And *Titanic* sank so quickly — in just two hours and 40 minutes — that there wasn't time for rescuers to reach the scene and save more people.

What *Titanic*'s owners and builders actually said was that their ship was '*practically* unsinkable', which is like saying they were 99.9% sure that it wouldn't sink, but couldn't totally guarantee it. Unfortunately, the ship became known as the Unsinkable Titanic, making them look very stupid indeed when it *did* sink.

Verdict : ___ **FICTION** ___

# Totally true Titanic facts

It was the first ship to have a heated swimming pool.

On their final evening, first-class passengers dined on oysters, roast squab, chocolate eclairs and seven other delicious courses.

Less than a minute elapsed between the first sighting of the iceberg and the impact.

# The sky is blue

Look at the sky on a lovely sunny day. There isn't a cloud above you and the sky is a bright blue. It's what you would see and what I would see. Except what we see might not actually be the truth of the matter.

## And the truth is...

Sunlight is, in fact, white. More remarkable still, this white light is actually the combination of lots of different colours: red, orange, yellow, green, blue, indigo and violet. This is called the spectrum and you see it every time you look at a rainbow — but what you are actually seeing is the light getting split up by water vapour.

The reason the sky looks blue is down to what's in the air. Our atmosphere is full of dust, gases and water vapour. All these different particles can scatter light — but blue light in particular. Of all the different colours it's the blue light that gets bounced around the most, and this is what we see when we look at the sky — bouncing blue light.

Verdict : — **FICTION** —

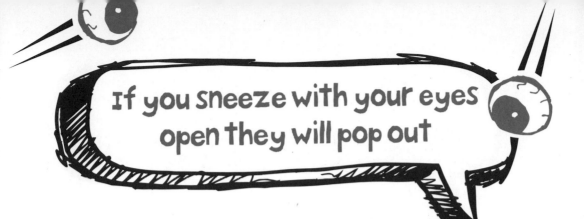

## If you sneeze with your eyes open they will pop out

A sneeze is a reaction to the nose being irritated and can help get rid of bacteria and germs. Sneezes can be pretty powerful, too — air gets pushed from your lungs and through your nose at up to 160 km/h (100 mph). That's a lot of force being generated and some people believe that this is why we close our eyes at the same time as we sneeze — because if we didn't our eyes would simply come flying out!

## ⭐ And the truth is...

Closing our eyes is simply a reaction and no one knows why we do it. There are plenty of people who can keep their eyes open when they sneeze and they aren't wandering about with their eyes hanging out. Give it a try yourself and see.

Verdict : ⎯ **FICTION** ⎯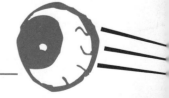

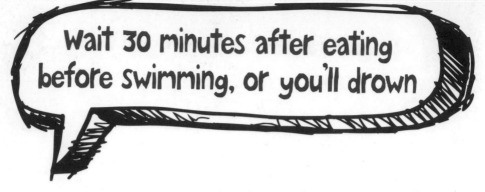

## Wait 30 minutes after eating before swimming, or you'll drown

This myth is a favourite with grandmothers and great aunts, and is a variation on, 'Let your food go down *before* you play football, go outside, strap on your rollerblades or even *think* about having any kind of fun.'

It's based on the idea that after you've eaten, your stomach needs oxygen to help it digest your food. But, of course, your muscles also need oxygen, and so if you go for a swim while your stomach's busy digesting food, the oxygen won't be available to your muscles. According to the myth, you'll be too weak to keep swimming and will, most likely, drown.

## ★ And the truth is...

In fact, your body takes in more than enough oxygen for movement *and* digestion. And as if that wasn't enough, your digestive system automatically shuts down within a minute or so after you start exercising.

## Verdict : ____  FICTION ____

No.1: The guillotine

Bonjour!

The guillotine sounds French, right? French revolutionaries certainly made this device famous when they started using it for chopping off people's heads in the 1790s. All in all, they managed to part at least 15,000 citizens from their *têtes*.

But despite being named after a Frenchman, Dr Guillotine, the chopping device was actually invented in Halifax, Yorkshire, in the UK. There, the 'Halifax Gibbet' was first used to execute criminals in 1286.

# When animals

# ATTACK!

## Escaping a bear

Think what it must be like for the bear. Every year, noisy hikers visit their woods and disturb the peace. The only thing worse is the smell of delicious food the hikers trail around after themselves. No wonder bears sometimes forget their manners and attack humans.

How can you stop it happening to you?

★ If the bear is 100 m or more away but has spotted you, start talking loudly but calmly. Once it realises you're human, it will probably leg it.

★ If it gets aggressive, don't run — you won't escape. Instead try to back slowly away, without looking the bear in the eye.

★ Climbing a tree may show the bear that you're not threatening it — but bears can climb trees too, so this won't be an escape.

# Head lice prefer clean hair

Sometimes, it seems you just can't win. You try and keep yourself looking clean and tidy, washing your hair every day. Then someone comes along and says:

*'You know head lice prefer clean hair, don't you? You're making it more likely you'll catch them.'*

In a way, this makes perfect sense. After all, if you were a head louse, where would you prefer to live? In a dirty, greasy forest of hair — or a lovely, clean, sweet-smelling one?

## ⭐ But the truth is...

Head lice set up home on your head in order to drink your blood. They have a mouth like a tiny sharp-ended straw, which they stick into your scalp and suck through. They clasp on to your hair near the skin, but they can clasp on to clean hair or dirty hair equally well — it doesn't make any difference to them!

Verdict :

# The Black Death killed half of Europe!

The Black Death was another name for the bubonic plague — a highly infectious disease carried by rats and fleas — that swept across Europe in 1348.

The plague was a seriously nasty way to die. The symptoms were painful swellings, called buboes. Victims also suffered from fever, vomiting, aches and pains, delirium and extreme sleepiness. It was called the Black Death because the skin around a bubo turned red, then purple and finally black.

Most who caught the Black Death were dead in days.

## ★ And the truth is...

There are no exact figures for the Black Death, but some historians think that the European mortality rate was about 50%. That's millions of people.

Verdict : _____ **FACT** (approximately)

## Cavemen fought with dinosaurs!

Ask any grown-up (preferably a slightly prehistoric one) and they'll tell you that they've seen stacks of films in which fur-clad cavemen — and cavewomen, too — fought dinosaurs. So this absolutely must be true, because film directors never make anything up.

## ★ And the truth is...

This never, ever, ever happened for the simple reason that the last of the dinosaurs lived in the Cretaceous period, while the first humans lived in the Paleolithic Era. And it wasn't as if these chunks of history were a few years or even centuries apart. The last dinosaurs were extinct *65 million years* before the first human appeared on Earth. So there's no way they could have met, let alone fought each other.

Film directors knew this, of course. But they also knew that dinosaurs plus humans equalled a box-office hit, so they bent the truth just a little. And who can blame them.

Verdict : ___Until time travel is invented___ **FICTION**

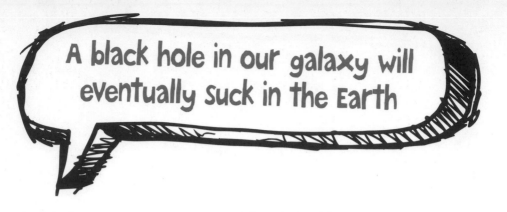

A black hole in our galaxy will eventually suck in the Earth

Black holes are mysterious, powerful and, frankly, very, very scary.
They are often the remains of stars that have died.
When a large star dies it erupts in a massive explosion called
a supernova. However, occasionally instead of exploding,
the centre of some massive stars implode — shrink down to
a tiny point. These remains can have the gravitational pull
of hundreds of Suns.

The largest black holes are called supermassive black holes and have
the gravity of millions of Sun-sized stars. Nothing can escape the pull
of a black hole — even light itself. And the bad news is that scientists
believe that there is a supermassive black hole at the centre of every
galaxy — including our own.

Our galaxy is called the Milky Way and the
supermassive black hole at its centre is
called Sagittarius A. Scientists think that
it has the same gravitational pull as
4 million Suns. Any nearby objects
might well be sucked in — and add
to the power of the black hole.

Help!

## ⭐ And the truth is...

The good news is that the Earth is probably too far away to get sucked in. The bad news is that there might well be a black hole scientists haven't spotted yet that is much closer. But the good news is that even if there is a closer one it still might not get us. But the bad news is the reason it won't get us is that in about 5 billion years scientists believe that the Sun will die and the Earth will be toast.

Verdict : ——— **FICTION** ———

It'll NEVER WORK!

'Heavier-than-air flying machines are impossible'

Lord Kelvin (1824-1907), British scientist and mathematician

## If you swallow an orange pip, an orange tree will grow inside you

One popular way for parents to frighten their children is to tell them that swallowing fruit seeds will cause a tree to grow inside their stomachs. Some even go so far as to say that the branches will eventually come out of their ears or mouth!

As well as scaring children, this myth puts them off eating fruit — which parents are always trying to get their kids to do. Which just goes to show how dumb some adults are.

The theory goes that plants need a) warmth and b) fluid. Since your insides are warm and full of fluid, the seed will germinate and grow into a plant.

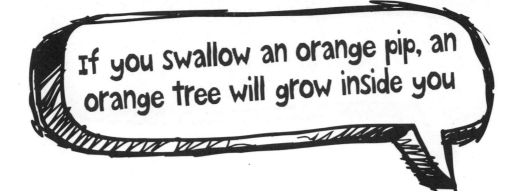

## ⭐ And the truth is...

Maybe this myth grew from the knowledge that some seeds are poisonous, so it's a bad idea to eat them.* But plants need light to grow — and if there's any light getting into your insides, there's *definitely* something wrong. Also, the juices in your stomach are acidic, and would kill a plant even if one *could* start growing.

Verdict : ——— **FICTION**   *See pages 46 and 47.

## An elephant never forgets

There's actually a much earlier version of this saying, from ancient Greece: *'A camel never forgets an injury.'* Today people say it's elephants that never forget, or that people with a good memory have, *'a memory like an elephant'.*

This idea is probably based on the fact that elephants have the biggest brain of any land animal. With all that brain, they must be using it for something, right? Surely little details like their mobile number or mum's birthday couldn't get lost in there?

### And the truth is...

Elephants are able to remember every detail of their home territory, especially things like where to find water, food or somewhere good to have a bath. They also remember the faces of other elephants. Years after seeing another elephant, they are able to recognise old friends immediately.

Verdict : _____ **FACT**

## Cheetahs are the world's fastest animals

Grown-ups love this fact, and will trot it out again and again. The cheetah can run at about 110 kph, which is pretty fast. It would be able to keep up in the fast lane of the motorway (though not quite fast enough to get a speeding ticket). Cheetahs can only keep at maximum speed for about 30 seconds — after that, they overheat and have to slow down.

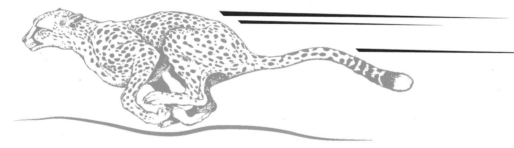

## ★ And the truth is...

Cheetahs are fast, but not the fastest. The peregrine falcon reaches speeds of about 320 kph as it dives down — or 'stoops' — after its prey. Of course, you might say that's cheeting (ha!), because the falcon has gravity helping it. But another bird, the spine-tailed swift, can fly at about 175 kph without help from gravity. That's plenty fast enough for a speeding ticket!

The cheetah is, though, the fastest land animal.

Verdict :  a bit true, but mostly **FICTION**

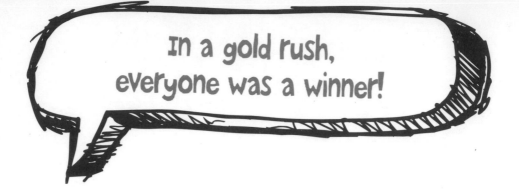

## In a gold rush, everyone was a winner!

Why else would gold prospectors spend years digging or crouched over a stream panning, if it wasn't because of guaranteed gold at the end of it?

Gold was discovered in California in 1848 and during the next seven years, about 300,000 prospectors from all around the world rushed there. (Because it was a gold rush. Get it?) But it was a hazardous journey by sea or by land. Those who made it to California found that panning for gold was tough work. Meanwhile, the poor Native Americans lost out big time when their land was overrun with prospectors.

## ⭐ And the truth is...

A very few prospectors *did* find enough gold to become stinking rich and some were lucky enough to make a small profit. But many gold prospectors spent more money rushing to the gold fields than they ever made from the gold they found there.

Verdict : **FICTION**

# BIG FILMS BAD SCIENCE

## Dinosaur Disasters

Even the biggest blockbusters get things horribly wrong. Take the *Jurassic Park* films for instance. They have fantastic computer generated images — but the science is a bit dodgy and an example of this is how the dinosaurs came to be alive today. A scientist was meant to have re-grown the dinosaurs from flies trapped in amber. The flies had bitten dinosaurs before they died and as a result had traces of dinosaur DNA inside them. DNA is like the code to what makes you unique. So the scientist took the DNA and grew dinosaurs from them.

This is wonky science because amber is great for preserving DNA — but not for millions and millions of years. Secondly the dinosaur DNA would have been mixed up with fly DNA so you wouldn't be able to separate the two strands.

**Verdict = extinct idea!**

## Chopping onions can make you weep

Sad films, miserable music, and dead pets are all pretty much guaranteed to make you weep — but a root vegetable?

## And the truth is...

The truth is that onions are more likely to bring tears to your eyes than slamming your head in a door. The reason lies in an evil mixture of chemicals inside the onion skin called amino acids and sulphurs. These are OK — unless you cut the onion. Then a fine gas with the tongue-tyingly long name of syn-Propanethial-S-oxide is transported through the air and into your eyes — promptly causing you to cry.

Avoid onion tears by wearing swim goggles near chopped onions. You will look like a wally, but at least you'll have dry eyes.

**FACT**

Verdict :_____

# You only use 10% of your brain

## There are several different versions of this myth:

**1**

You only use 10% of your brain

Apparently, researchers have hooked people up to machines that provide an image of what their brain is doing. The bits where there's something going on light up in colour. Amazingly, when they ask people to think about something or perform an action, it's clear that only 10% of the brain is being used!

Ten per cent?
As much as that?

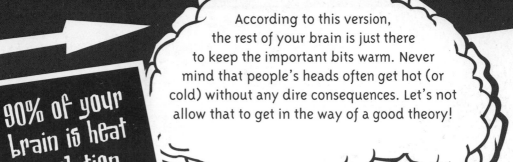

**2**

**90% of your brain is heat insulation**

According to this version, the rest of your brain is just there to keep the important bits warm. Never mind that people's heads often get hot (or cold) without any dire consequences. Let's not allow that to get in the way of a good theory!

This theory says that the extra 90% is actually used for activities that science cannot measure. Stuff like communicating with the dead, predicting the future or sensing danger. Of course, whenever you hear about things science cannot measure, it's time to watch out. If science can't measure it, it's generally because it doesn't exist…

**3**

**90% of your brain is used in mysterious ways**

## ★ And the truth is…

In fact, you *do* use only about 10% of your brain at any one time — but that's not the same as saying the other 90% is never used. We use different bits of our brains for different things, and not all of them are used at the same time.

Verdict : ___a bit true — but mainly___ 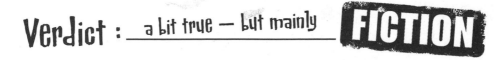 **FICTION**

## Weeing on a jellyfish sting will cure it

There are few things worse than going for a lovely swim on a hot day, then being stung by a jellyfish. (Seeing a shark's fin appear alongside you is one of them — see pages 80-81 for ideas on how to get out of *that* situation.)

A jellyfish sting happens when you brush against its tentacles. These are armed with stingers, which pierce your skin and inject venom. The pain happens straight away, and can be very bad.

Someone's bound to tell you that the cure for the sting is for someone to wee on it. But even if the pain's so bad you're tempted to agree — will it work?

### ⭐ The truth is...

Wee won't help, and could make it worse.
The chemical make-up of wee will probably cause the stingers left on your skin to release more venom. For most stings, the best treatment is to wash it down with seawater.

Verdict:  **FICTION**

# ⭐ 5 things you (probably) didn't know about CAMELS

**1** Camels can't live without water for as long as giraffes …

**2** … or rats.

**3** Camels like company, which is why they hang out in herds.

**4** When they are angry, scared or frustrated, camels spit. The rotten juice they gob at you comes up from their stomach.

**5** Camels have the biggest mouths of any ruminants*, so they can give a nasty bite.

*Hoofed mammals that chew mainly grass, and have several chambers in their stomach

# Five Ancient Olympic truths

1. Boxers were allowed to carry on biffing and bashing their opponents, even after they were down and out.

2. Ancient Olympian runners did not get on their marks before a race. They stood up very straight, with their arms stretched out in front of them.

3. The hoplitodromos event was not a tongue-twister game but a running race in which a competitor ran in full battle gear (including armour and shield).

4. The winner of an event was presented with an olive branch, not a gold medal. Wow.

5. The last Ancient Olympics took place around the 4th century AD. Fans then had to hang on another 1,500 years for the Modern Olympics to begin. They must have been dead tired of waiting.

Things they never said

'Elementary, my dear Watson.'

This is probably one of Sherlock Holmes' most famous lines. But it doesn't appear in any of Sir Arthur Conan Doyle's novels about the fictional detective.

## Air doesn't weigh anything

Sometimes things are described as being 'as light as air' meaning they have practically no weight at all. After all we are surrounded by air and we can't feel it weighing down on us. Look at a set of weighing scales — they won't show any weight from the air above it. So air can't weigh anything, right?

100% AIR

### ★ And the truth is...

Air weighs an awful lot. If you draw a square one metre by one metre on the ground the air above the square actually weighs around 9,000 kg (8.9 tons) — that's around 11 elephants' worth. The higher you go above sea level, the less the air will weigh because there will be less of it above you.

For life to flourish on this planet it has to adapt to the weight of the air above it. If we weren't designed to cope with the weight we'd be as flat as pancakes. The fact that we don't feel the weight is because we're used to it and are built to withstand it.

Verdict :  **FICTION**

# There is more caffeine in tea than coffee

Tea and coffee both contain a substance called caffeine. This substance acts as a stimulant — it gives you a boost of energy. It's so effective a stimulant that athletes were banned from using it before competitions. However, too much caffeine is bad for you and can leave you feeling jittery, stressed and might stop you from sleeping. In very extreme cases it could kill you.

*I say, I'm buzzin'*

*Awesome!*

## ★ And the truth is...

Caffeine is present in many drinks and foods like chocolate. However the largest amounts are in tea and coffee. The amount varies depending on which type of tea or coffee you choose, but generally a cup of coffee has more caffeine than a cup of tea. Interestingly though, a portion of tea leaves has more caffeine than a portion of coffee grains — when boiling water is added to the leaves it reduces the amount of caffeine.

Verdict : **FACT** and **FICTION**

*but mainly fiction*

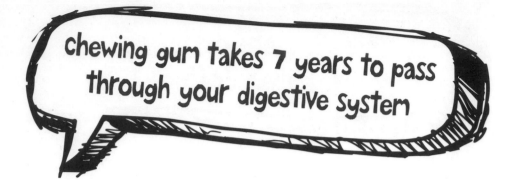

chewing gum takes **7** years to pass through your digestive system

Most of us have been told this by our parents at some time or another. Another version of the saying goes that the sticky gum will wrap itself around your internal organs and may even clog up your insides!

The thinking behind the chewing gum warnings goes like this:

> *Chewing gum isn't food – and you shouldn't swallow things that aren't food, right?*

> *Chewing gum's sticky: once it's inside you, it will just stick to your insides and take ages to come out.*

## ★ And the truth is...

Chewing gum isn't especially sticky after you've swallowed it, and there's no special reason why it should a) take a long time to pass through your digestive system or b) get wrapped around your organs.

People have had the chewing habit for hundreds of years — in fact since long before chewing gum was even invented. (Before gum, people used to chew tree resin.) Humans have *always* chewed resin or gum, and they've probably *always* swallowed it from time to time.

Verdict : ____ **FICTION** ___

# You can cook an egg with two mobile phones

The instructions for anyone wanting to do this (no one ever explains *why* you'd want to cook an egg using mobile phones) are as follows:

1. *Place an uncooked egg between two mobile phones, with the phones facing each other.*

2. *Call one phone from the other. Nothing will happen for the first 15 minutes (except for your call charges racking up). After that, the egg starts to cook.*

3. *After 65 minutes, end the call, then break the egg open. You will find that it's cooked.*

## ★ And the truth is...

When mobile phones first appeared on the scene, there were all kinds of scare stories about them. Some people even claimed they would fry your brain. This particular story was cooked up (ha!) in 2000 as a spoof.

Verdict :  **FICTION**

# I'd never have known...

**Lobsters grow slowly, and can live a very long time. Most of the lobsters people eat are about 20 years old, but there are some real old giants crawling around on the seabed.**

The oldest lobsters are probably over 100 years old, and weigh about the same as a medium-sized dog.

Talking of which, the French poet Gérard de Nerval had a pet lobster called Thibault. He used to take it for walks around Paris!

# one dog year equals seven human ones

People will often tell you that to work out how old a dog is in human terms, you should multiply its age by seven. So, a 3-year-old poodle would be 21 in human terms. A 9-year-old Labrador would be 63, and just thinking about retirement.

ROVER

## ⭐ And the truth is...

This myth is based on the idea that dogs live one-seventh as long as humans — about 11 years. Bigger pedigree dogs, such as Labradors and Alsatians, do live about this long. Smaller dogs and non-pedigrees usually live longer, and many make it to 15 years or more. Using the seven-year rule, a 15-year-old dog would be 105 in human years.

Verdict : _____ mostly  **FICTION**

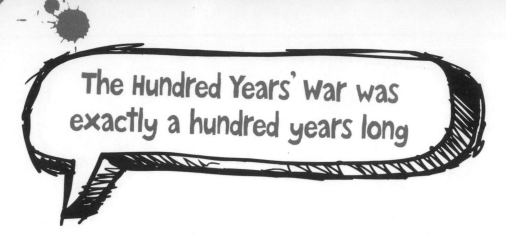

## The Hundred Years' War was exactly a hundred years long

Imagine that. A hundred years of non-stop fighting... Except, the Hundred Years' War wasn't just one war, but several battles that took place between the House of Valois (France) and the House of Plantagenet (England).

The English king, Edward III, started it all. When his uncle, Charles IV of France died, he thought that he should become king of France too. But the French wanted Charles' cousin Philip to be king. So they fought. And fought. Again and again and again. When the kings died, it didn't even signal an end to the fighting. Their successors simply carried on the war.

The Battle of Agincourt, starring Henry V, was one of the most famous battles of the Hundred Years' War. But there were many more. And by the time it was over, Edward III had been dead for 76 years.

Who won? The French. When the war was over, the English had lost all of their French territory apart from the port of Calais.

## ⭐ And the truth is...

The Hundred Years' War lasted from 1337 to 1453, which made it 116 years long. So, unless you have a very dodgy calculator, the Hundred Years' War... um... wasn't. In fact, it was a name thought up by historians, who presumably couldn't add up, much later.

Verdict : **FICTION**

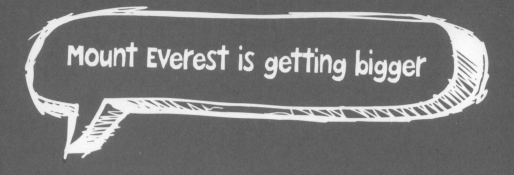

# Mount Everest is getting bigger

Mountains look like they've been around since the beginning of time; but the simple fact is that they haven't and the reason why lies in the way the Earth's surface is made. The surface isn't one solid piece; it's actually made up of big pieces like a massive jigsaw. These pieces are called plates, and the plates move about. They don't move very quickly — just a few centimetres a year — but over millions of years the world looks very different now to how it used to.

Another result of the plates moving is that mountains are made. Often when two plates meet, one plate slides underneath the other; but sometimes they hit and they crunch up a bit. The ripples become mountain ranges.

## ⭐ And the truth is...

Mount Everest is part of the Himalayan mountain range, which was formed when two plates crunched into each other. They're still crashing into each other today and as a result Mount Everest is growing at around 6cm (2 in) per year.

Verdict: ———————— FACT ———

# Eating apple pips can poison you!

We all know stories about people (usually princesses) being poisoned or sent to sleep by apples. But they're just fairy stories, right? Even so, people will still insist to you that you really mustn't eat apple pips, because they contain poison.

Yes, it's the pips that can hurt you!

46

You might even hear someone saying that cherry stones, or the pits of peaches and apricots, are poisonous too. Of course, this must be nonsense: things millions of people eat every day can't be poisonous. Can they?

 ## And the truth is...

Apple pips contain a substance called amygdalin. When this is digested, it turns into hydrogen cyanide. (Hydrogen cyanide is the deadly chemical the Nazis used to kill people in concentration camps during the Second World War.)

The good news is that apple pips have a hard outer shell, which means they normally pass through your insides without being digested. Plus, you'd have to eat literally TONNES of apples to be poisoned.

Cherry stones, as well as peach and apricot pits also contain amygdalin. Of course, these come with a rock-hard protective outer layer, which would be rather uncomfortable to swallow. But the pits of peaches and apricots do contain enough amygdalin to be harmful.

Verdict : _____ mostly

# I'd never have known...

**Rodents such as mice make a tasty snack for a hungry fox — and they have a brilliant technique for catching them.**

The fox leaps up in the air (up to about a metre), and comes down vertically towards the mouse. Either:

 **a**    The mouse jumps upwards, straight into the fox's mouth, or;

**b**    The fox uses its paws to pin the mouse down, stunning it and enabling the fox to sink its teeth in!

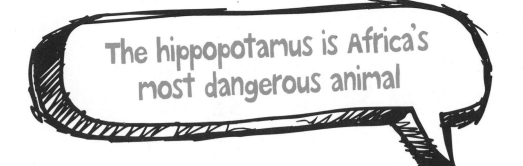

# The hippopotamus is Africa's most dangerous animal

Africa is full of dangerous animals: deadly black mamba snakes*, giant Nile crocodiles, lions, leopards, etc, etc. But the most dangerous one might come as a surprise: it's the bumbling old hippopotamus.

Hippos aren't quite as harmless as they first seem. For a start, their mouths have huge teeth, up to half a metre long. They're easily capable of biting off a man's head as he cowers in a hole, trying to hide.

Get between a hippo and the water — especially if it's a mother hippo with young swimming about — and the adult hippo can be very aggressive. And males are always aggressive if you wander into their territory.

 **And the facts are...**

All true. You'll know if a hippo gets annoyed, because it will start to sweat red sticky stuff. Knowing it's annoyed probably won't do you much good, though — despite looking a bit hefty, hippos can run at over 30 kph.

Verdict : _____

*See page 56 for a bit more about these.

# CELEBRITY
# GOSSIP
## from long ago

Napoleon Boneparte (1769-1821) is famous for being a French emperor and a great military leader. But he was also rumoured to be a very short man. (So what? His achievements — before the Battle of Waterloo ended his career — were huge!)

Anyway, the story goes that a doctor measured Napoleon's height in 1802 and said that he was 5 feet and 2 inches tall, which is about 1.57 metres. So that's it sorted then. He was really short. But, er, hang on a minute. What about the small matter of the old French inch being just a bit bigger than the standard measurement? When Napoleon's height was measured, a French inch actually equalled 2.7 cm, while a standard inch is just 2.54 cm. This might not sound like much of a difference until his height is converted in metric. Instead of being 1.57 metres tall, his height suddenly rockets to 1.7 metres tall, which is roughly 5 feet 7 inches. So, in fact, three centuries ago, this would have made him taller than average. Which makes the fact that he was short a <u>very</u> tall story.

Surely not? Just the thought of washing clothes in smelly old wee is enough to make someone wrinkle up their nose. But it's said that in medieval times — and even as far back as the Ancient Romans — people used wee to remove stubborn stains from their clothes.

## ★ And the truth is...

Well, they had to use something, didn't they? Washing powder hadn't yet been invented and wee — or urine, to use its proper name — contains ammonia, which is very good at getting things clean.

In Ancient Rome, launderers left buckets on street corners for passers-by to stop and 'go'. And when they'd collected enough liquid, the launderers diluted it with water, then popped in the clothes and left them to soak. They might even ask a helper or a slave to stomp on the clothes to get them really clean.

Verdict : _____

# The Earth is closest to the Sun in summer

It's easy to forget that our lovely planet, Earth, is really just a rock spinning through space. It's not just hurtling in any random direction of course, it goes round and round our star, the Sun, taking a year to complete each trip round. And it's thanks to the Sun that we get all our natural heat and light.

The path we take around the Sun isn't a true circle; instead it's an ellipse, which is a bit like an oval. This means that the distance Earth is from the Sun varies — sometimes it's nearer and sometimes it's further away. It makes sense then, that when we are closer to the Sun we have summer and when we are further away we have winter.

## ⭐ And the truth is...

When the northern hemisphere (the bit we think of as being above the equator) has its summer it's actually at its furthest from the Sun. How? The answer is down to the fact that the Earth is on the wonk; it doesn't sit straight, in fact it leans over by 23°. This means as the Earth travels round the Sun one half of the world leans closer for one half of the year and then the other half leans closer for the second half. The half that leans closer has summer. If the Earth was straight, both the northern and southern hemispheres would have summer at the same time.

Verdict :———— **FICTION** —

# on average, women swallow 2-4 kg of lipstick during their lifetime

When women put on lipstick, many of them rub their lips together to 'bed it in'. The story goes that a little bit of it always ends up in their mouth, and then gets swallowed. More lipstick can get swallowed while licking lips, eating and drinking. Incredibly, during a woman's lifetime, she will end up swallowing at least 2 kg of the stuff!

This myth has been reported in newspapers and magazines all round the world, from Australia to the UK, Canada and the USA.

## ★ And the truth is...

A stick of lipstick weighs 2–3 g. So even the lowest estimate — 2 kg — would be 667 whole sticks of lipstick. To reach 4 kg, a woman would have to swallow 1,334 entire sticks. Both these figures seem unlikely.

Say you get 200 applications from a stick: 667 sticks equals about 133,400 applications. A woman who starts wearing lipstick at 15 and stops at 65 has 18,262.5 possible days of lipstick-wearing in between. She'd have to be putting on a fresh coat of lippie 7 or 8 times a day, every day, even to USE 2 kg of lipstick — let alone swallow it.

Verdict :  **FICTION**

# Where In The World?

Most people think that poodles come from France, but they're actually German. Their name comes from the German word 'pudelhund'.

Poodles were bred partly for swimming, and some people claim that their strange pom-pom haircuts were intended to keep their joints warm while in the water.

# YOU SHOULD SUCK VENOM OUT OF SNAKEBITES

At one time, scenes based on this idea appeared in just about every adventure movie/Western/war film. At some point, a snake would bite somebody. Usually it was a rattlesnake, but sometimes a black mamba. (This is one of the world's deadliest snakes, able to kill a grown elephant — or several humans — with its venom.)

In the movies, when someone is bitten by a snake the following procedure has to be followed:

1. Tie a tourniquet around the leg that's been bitten.
2. Slice the bite open with a knife.
3. Suck out the venom into your mouth
4. Spit it out.
5. Rinse out your mouth with water; spit again; say, 'He'll be OK now' as the victim falls backwards with relief.

So, if you happen to be bitten by a venomous* snake, would this be a good way to react?

*Venoms are harmful when injected into your flesh; poisons are harmful if swallowed or breathed in. That's why biting snakes are called 'venomous', and why in theory it would be safe to suck venom out of a bite.

## ⭐ The truth is...

You are unlikely to be able to suck any venom from the snakebite. Trying it is not likely to do you any harm — but if there are cuts inside your mouth, the venom could enter your body through these.

The best treatment for snakebite is to keep the victim calm and still, which stops their heart beating fast and spreading the venom quickly round their body. Call the emergency services as soon as possible.

Verdict : __ **FICTION** __

# A WEE HISTORY OF THE WORLD

## 1. The Aztecs used wee to disinfect wounds.

Wee is reasonably sterile, so it makes sense. But many experts say that it's really not a good idea and it is actually much better to use antiseptic cream.

## 2. Wee-soaked cloth makes a fabulous DIY gas mask.

In the First World War, soldiers actually did this if they didn't have a gas mask with them. The urine protected them against a chlorine attack. Phew-y!

## 3. Wee makes an excellent invisible ink.

Ask any spy (if you can find one, that is) and they'll tell you that wee is far easier to carry than a bottle of invisible ink. A message written in wee can be later revealed by heating up the paper it's written on.

## 4. Diluted wee is used by art experts to restore old masterpieces.

Ha ha! This is not true (but it sounds good, doesn't it?).

## 5. Wee is a teeth-whitener.

Forget the cosmetic dentist. Ancient Romans used wee to make their smiles as white and bright as A-list celebrities. Ting!

## 6. If you pick a dandelion, you will wet the bed.

The green leaves of a dandelion do actually act as a diuretic, which means that they make you wee more. But picking them has absolutely no effect on a person's bladder whatsoever. In fact, Native Americans used dandelion leaves to cure heartburn, indigestion and constipation.

# Deserts are <u>always</u> really, really hot

We all have a clear idea of what a desert looks like: hot, sandy, barren — a wilderness stretching for miles on end, frying under the relentless, burning sun. Deserts cover over one fifth of the land across the world and are actually home to a wide range of plants and animals. They have adapted to live in dry desert conditions; even in places like the Atacama desert which might not see rain for years and years at a time.

## ★ And the truth is...

The important word in the last paragraph was 'dry'. A desert is any place that receives less than 50 cm (19.6 in) of rainfall in a year. This might mean the type of desert described above, or cold dry regions. Antarctica, for example gets very little fresh rain or snow, so is actually classed as a desert.

Verdict : **FICTION**

# fatty foods are good for you

Eh? what? If you eat fatty foods you will get fat; or worse still suffer from a whole range of health problems such as heart disease. But there are lots of different sorts of fats, so try getting your mouth around these (er, ok...perhaps not all of them): saturated, monounsaturated, polyunsaturated, and trans fats. Are they all bad for us?

 ## And the truth is...

The good news is that we need a certain amount of fat to survive. And that list of fats can be split into good fats and bad fats. Monounsaturated and polyunsaturated fats are generally good fats. They are found in things like salmon, or olive oil for example. So a diet that has these fats in is going to be good for you. Of course, as with all diet advice, don't eat too much of anything to be properly healthy. Too much good fat is bad for you too!

Verdict : **FACT** and **FICTION**

> # A special chemical in swimming pools turns red if you wee in the water

Imagine this: you're swimming along happily, and suddenly people swimming around you start to scream and head for the edges of the pool. A cloud of red appears around you in the water. Has a shark somehow got into the pool and bitten you? Of course not! You've done a naughty wee, and Urine Alert Dye™ has made the water go red.

Adults like to warn young people at every opportunity about the special chemical in swimming pools that turns red (or sometimes green or blue) if someone does a wee in the water. The idea is so popular that it's even made it into the movies, in the 2010 film *Grown Ups*. But is the story true?

## ★ And the truth is...

Urine Alert Dye™ doesn't exist. In fact, it would probably be almost impossible to make. You'd need to find something in wee for the dye to react with. But any chemical in wee would probably also be in the pool from other sources, such as sweat, so the water would constantly be red. This is a story put about by lifeguards and parents to keep kids in line.

Verdict: ——  **FICTION** ——

## Weeing on a live rail will electrocute you

Weeing in the pool is embarrassing (as well as being a revolting thing to do), but it won't actually *kill* you. But the saying goes that if you wee on a live train track, you won't have the luxury of being embarrassed — you'll be dead! Which would come as a nasty shock, even to someone dumb enough to go anywhere NEAR a live train line...

The idea is that, because electricity passes through water, the power of the rail will zip up the stream of wee and hit your body. You'll quickly be doing an impression of a dead person — except it won't be an impression.

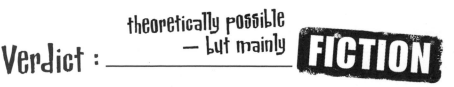

## ★ And the truth is...

In theory this is possible, so DON'T TRY IT. But in practice, it would be very unlikely. Almost as soon as it starts to come out, the stream of wee begins to break up into drops, with air gaps between them. Electricity would not pass along this. So to be electrocuted you'd have to be crouching SO close to the rail that you'd be almost touching it — which would be pretty dumb.

Verdict : _____ theoretically possible — but mainly **FICTION**

## Kangaroos are good at boxing

Boxing kangaroos are a symbol of Australian pride. During the Second World War they were painted as symbols on Australian fighter planes and ships. Today, the Australian Olympic team uses the boxing kangaroo image. But are kangaroos actually any good at boxing?

⭐ **The truth is...**

In the late 1900s, travelling shows gave men the chance to box against kangaroos in the ring. The men rarely, if ever, won. Male kangaroos* box each other over females or access to drinking spots. They grapple with their smaller front paws, and make powerful kicks with their back paws.

Verdict : _____

*The name for a group of kangaroos is a 'mob'.

# 5 things you (probably) didn't know about CROCODILES

**1** Crocodiles can run at speeds of up to 17 kph, but only for short distances. However ...

**2** ... they can launch themselves out of the water at speeds of up to 40 kph.

**3** A crocodile's bite is 12 times more powerful than a great white shark's.

**4** Crocodiles have very weak jaw-opening muscles. It's possible to tape their jaws shut with packing tape.

**5** The bigger the pool, the bigger the croc it will hold. Crocodiles never outgrow the pool in which they live.

## The Ancient Olympians raced in the nude!

The very first Olympic Games took place in 776 BC. Dedicated to Zeus, king of the Greek gods, there was only one event — a running race, but it soon became a major sporting occasion, including the long jump, javelin, discus, wrestling, boxing and chariot racing. But forget technical sportswear. Sporty types in Ancient Greece competed in their birthday suits — they wore *nothing at all*.

ATHENS

### ⭐ And the truth is...

Ancient athletes really *did* compete naked, but no one is entirely sure why. One theory is that a runner's loincloth slipped and he tripped, so clothes were considered a safety hazard and removed. Others think that the Greeks just liked the human body — there are plenty of scantily clad statues, after all — and wanted to admire the sportsmen as they competed. It might have been a tribute to the gods.

Or perhaps it was just because the weather was hot. Whatever the reason, this was something that just the male athletes did. Women did not compete and married women weren't even allowed in the stadium to be spectators.

Verdict : _____ 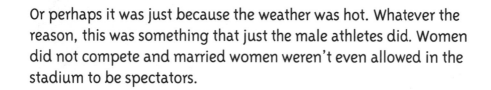 _____

FACT

# Human beings go POP in space

Human beings need a few things to survive: food, water and air being the basics. The most immediately important of the three is air and unfortunately for us, this can't be found in space (food and water are pretty scarce too). Space is near enough a vacuum, which means there is nothing there, no gas, no matter, nada, zilch, nothing. This has led people to suppose that because there is air pressure inside your body, it would make the body swell like a balloon and explode.

## ★ And the truth is...

The fact that our body is wrapped in skin stops us from exploding – our skin is strong enough to deal with the pressure. So although everything on your inside might want to get to the outside your skin keeps it all where it should be. After a few seconds in space without the correct gear you would pass out from lack of oxygen and eventually die – but you wouldn't explode.

Verdict :  **FICTION**

# BIG FILMS BAD SCIENCE

The movies are great for entertainment but the absolute pits for science!

## Star Flaws

Films set in space are known as science fiction and yet the science bits are rubbish. You could say that generally the science is purely erm… fiction. Take all those wonderful space ships for example, whooshing and zooming through space with those fantastic space ship noises. Except that's exactly the trouble — you can't hear anything in space (see page 100 to find out why), so spaceships just wouldn't make those noises.

Or take those ray guns, shooting those colourful laser beams with some devastating results. Except that's not how lasers work — for a start they don't come in all those great colours. In real life you can't see them. So you can't dodge out of the way of them. Lasers move at the speed of light — which is the fastest anything can move — so no matter how quickly you duck it won't be fast enough.

And don't get us started on lightsabers.

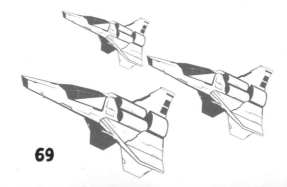

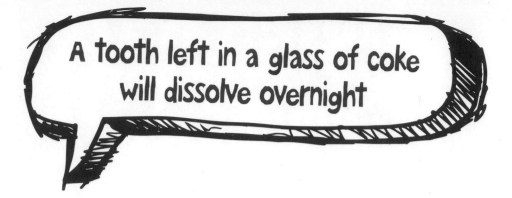

# A tooth left in a glass of coke will dissolve overnight

This is a favourite of grown-ups who are trying to explain why you don't need another fizzy drink. There are other versions, including the story of a piece of meat, left in a glass of Coke overnight, which had completely dissolved by the morning. It's also been claimed that there's something in Coke that will clean coins, and even eat away at marble steps!

## ★ And the truth is...

This myth started when a university professor told the US government that a tooth left in a glass of Coke would *begin* to soften and dissolve in 2 days. He blamed the sugar and phosphoric acid the drink contains. It's true that these can rot teeth, but it takes a long time. After you drink Coke, your saliva washes away most of the sugar and acid, preventing your teeth from rotting away. Anything remaining is brushed off when you clean your teeth (which you do twice a day, don't you?).

Verdict :  **FICTION**

> ## orange juice is bad for your teeth

**This sounds crazy, right?**
The idea that something as healthy as orange juice could rot your teeth is just ridiculous.

But then again…

★ **The truth is…**
Remember the sugar and phosphoric acid in Coke on page 70? Well, there's a lot more of it in orange juice. In fact, there's almost twice as much of the acid in orange juice as in Coke.

This acid eats into the surface of your teeth, making them slightly softer than usual. Normally this isn't a big problem, because your teeth harden again in about an hour. But if you brush your teeth just after drinking orange juice (or other fruit juices), you're actually brushing away the protective layer. Eventually your teeth will rot away, and you'll look like a toothless character in a fairy tale. Yuck.

Verdict : ———————— mostly **FACT**

# TIGERS HAVE

This sounds unlikely, doesn't it? Everyone knows tigers have stripy fur, not skin. That's what makes a tiger a tiger, after all. Whether it's a Siberian tiger, a Bengal tiger, a Sumatran tiger, or some other kind, they all have stripy fur.

# STRIPY SKIN

⭐ ### The truth is...

It would have been a brave person who first shaved a live tiger to discover this, but a tiger's pattern of black stripes is indeed contained on its skin, as well as its fur.

Verdict : **FACT**

> ## Sir Isaac Newton discovered gravity when an apple fell on his head

It's a lovely story and it goes something like this...

Once upon a time, Sir Isaac Newton was leaning against a tree and pondering the laws of physics, when suddenly an apple fell from the tree above him and landed on his head. *Bop*. 'Goodness gracious me,' thought Newton, rubbing his crown. 'If gravity can make an apple fall from a tree to the ground, perhaps it works over greater distances — maybe as far away as the Moon? Wow. I must think of a theory to explain that.' So he did. And he called it Newton's law of universal gravitation.

The End.

## ⭐ And the truth is...

A piece of fruit never fell on Newton's head. But we know that he *did* watch an apple fall from a tree, and that this made him think about gravity, because he told people about it. And he did come up with his law of universal gravitation. So whether the apple fell on his head or not doesn't matter. It still made him think.

Verdict : _____ a little bit TRUE, but mostly **FICTION**

# A baby can become a genius by listening to Mozart

In 1993 scientists made a surprising discovery. They found that by playing music by the famous Austrian composer Wolfgang Amadeus Mozart people performed better in mental tests than people who had listened to different music or none at all. The findings became known as 'the Mozart effect'. A similar trial was conducted on pre-school children, and they too seemed to perform better after exposure to Mozart. Logically, it made sense that playing music to both unborn and newborn babies would also be beneficial.

## ★ And the truth is...

'The Mozart effect' is very controversial. Some scientists have been unable to replicate the results. Also, the effect itself wears off after 12–15 minutes (though longer for children). Worse still, one of the scientists from the original experiment also suggested later that there was no evidence that it would make babies more intelligent. So you can put the Mozart CD away now Mum.

Verdict :  **FICTION**

## Water goes down the plug hole in different directions north or south of the equator

The Earth rotates which is why we get night and day. However that is not the only effect this rotation has. It is also responsible for weather patterns which is due to something called the Coriolis effect. This is a complicated theory that concerns how objects move and it's often given as the reason why water spins down the plug hole in different directions north or south of the equator.

## ★ And the truth is...

The direction water spins as it goes down the plug hole has more to do with a whole range of different factors, such as: the way the sink is made, the direction the water was already moving before the plug is pulled, and how the plug is pulled. The Coriolis effect is way too small to have any noticeable effect.

Verdict : _____ **FICTION**

# Sports inventions you probably haven't heard of before

Ever heard the phrase: 'The answer to a question no one was asking'? The lack of success for these wacky sports inventions suggests they might fit that description:

## 1 Wings for skiers

A crazy contraption to be used instead of ski poles; the wings were attached to a harness worn by the skier. He or she could use them to 'create lift.'

## 2 The jet-powered surfboard

More than one attempt has been made to build a jet-powered or motorised surfboard. Ideal for surfers who for some reason are unable to paddle — perhaps because they're too busy strumming their ukuleles?

WOOAAAA

# It'll NEVER HAPPEN!

'It will be years — not in my time — before a woman will become Prime Minister.'

Margaret Thatcher speaking in 1969, ten years before becoming Prime Minister of the UK. As you can probably tell from the fact that her name was Margaret, Mrs T was herself a woman!

# When animals

# ATTACK!

**So, you're out for a swim and you see the thing everyone dreads — a fin rising up and starting to circle you. The music from *Jaws* starts up in your head —** *duuh dun... duuh dun... dun dun, dun dun, dundun, dundun, dundundundundundundundun.*

How do you avoid becoming a great white lunch?

★ Keep the shark in sight. Your best chance of surviving is to beat off the attack, if it comes.

★ Shout, or wave your arms over your head, to attract help from nearby boats or the shore.

★ Great whites like to attack into the sun. If the shark disappears, it is likely to emerge from below towards the sun shining on the surface. Check beneath you!

★ Fight back if the shark comes close enough — attack its eyes and gills, as this may force it to think again.

# GOSSIP

## Julius Caesar was born by Caesarean section

A Caesarean section is an operation performed on a pregnant woman, usually when a natural birth would put her or the unborn baby at risk. A cut is made in the woman's abdomen, the baby is pulled out and the woman is stitched up, as good as new. (Well, that's the straightforward explanation, anyway. Any surgeon will tell you that it's a bit trickier than that.)

It's often claimed that the operation is named Caesarean because the Roman emperor Julius Caesar was born that way. But in Roman times, the operation meant certain death for the mother … and Caesar's mother was very much alive after he was born. In fact, she lived long enough to become one of his advisors. ('Caesarean' is more likely to come from the Latin verb *caedere*, which means 'to cut'.)

> ## Ancient Egyptians had their noses chopped off if they didn't pay tax!

It seems a pretty extreme punishment for tax evasion, doesn't it? A fine, maybe, but chopping off someone's nose because they didn't pay their taxes sounds *totally* mad.

## ★ And the truth is...

Ancient Egyptians whose noses or ears were removed got off lightly. At least they were still alive. Anyone who stole cattle was impaled (see Vlad the Impaler on pages 162–163 for a bloodthirsty explanation of what *this* was) and then his wife and children were forced into slavery. As for grave robbers, they were tortured or killed. It was up to the pharaoh to decide whether they would be drowned, beheaded or burned alive. Goodness, he was spoilt for choice.

Verdict : _____

# RADIATION CAN GIVE YOU SUPERPOWERS

It must be great being a superhero; you could fly, or have laser beam eyes, or the strength of fifty men. The only downside is you have to wear a silly costume with your underpants on top of your trousers. But how do you get to be a superhero?

Often superheroes get their super-skills in some surprising ways. See if you can match these superheroes to the method they got their powers.

## SUPERHEROES

★ *Spiderman*

★ *The Hulk*

★ *The Fantastic Four*

★ *Daredevil*

★ *Captain America*

## METHOD

★ **Gamma rays from an experiment that went wrong**

★ **Drinks a special formula and is exposed to 'vita-rays'**

★ **Bitten by radioactive spider**

★ **Exposed to radioactive material as a child**

★ **Flew through a cloud of cosmic radiation**

**Answers:**

Spiderman got bitten by a radioactive spider; the Hulk got his strength when he was exposed to too much radiation in an experiment that went wrong; the Fantastic Four flew through the cloud; Daredevil was exposed to radioactive material as a child and Captain America drank the formula and had the 'vita-rays'.

They all became superheroes, so radiation must be the answer!

## And the truth is...

We are exposed to radiation all the time, but in very low doses so we don't notice. Radiation comes from the ground and from space; it even comes from mobile phones. Coming into contact with a large dose of radiation *would* have an effect — it would probably kill you. At the very least it would give you radiation sickness and a whole host of unpleasant symptoms such as vomiting, diarrhoea, gum disease and hair loss.

There's a good reason that superheroes only exist in comic books — in real life they'd be dead.

Verdict : _____  **FICTION**

Blonde people are slowly going to die out

The basis of this idea is that the gene determining hair colour is weaker in blonde people (or ginger-haired people) than in dark-haired people. So if a blonde person and a dark-haired person have children, the children will have dark hair more often than not. The only way for blondes to survive is to have children only with other blondes. But ridiculously, given that their very survival is at stake, they keep getting together with *dark*-haired people!

## ⭐ And the truth is...

There's no actual evidence for any of this. The research is often said to have come from the World Health Organization, but they deny any knowledge of it. So this must be a story made up by someone who wishes they had blonde hair, but doesn't.

Verdict :  **FICTION**

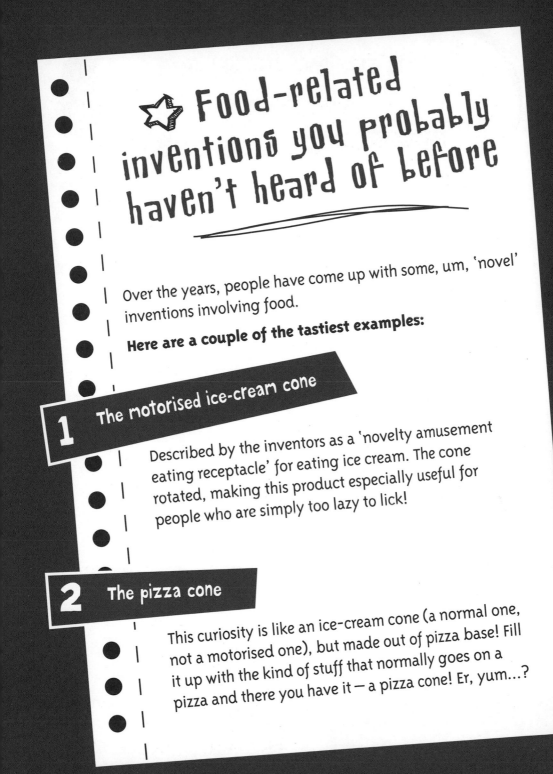

# Food-related inventions you probably haven't heard of before

Over the years, people have come up with some, um, 'novel' inventions involving food.

**Here are a couple of the tastiest examples:**

## 1 The motorised ice-cream cone

Described by the inventors as a 'novelty amusement eating receptacle' for eating ice cream. The cone rotated, making this product especially useful for people who are simply too lazy to lick!

## 2 The pizza cone

This curiosity is like an ice-cream cone (a normal one, not a motorised one), but made out of pizza base! Fill it up with the kind of stuff that normally goes on a pizza and there you have it — a pizza cone! Er, yum...?

# You swallow spiders in your sleep!

And what's more, we apparently swallow eight spiders a year.

Few people are loony enough to pick up a spider and gulp it down while they're awake. The idea is that as you lie there drooling on your pillow, spiders can approach and crawl in. Three main reasons for the spiders' attraction to the mouths of sleeping humans have been put forward:

**1** One report says that spiders are attracted by the smell of rotten food between your teeth (if true, this is a very good reason to floss regularly!)

**2** Others suggest that the vibrations of people snoring have a fatal attraction for spiders.

**3** Some people think the spiders are just looking for a quiet place to rest. This does rather disagree with the snoring theory, but never mind... zzzzz.

## ⭐ And the facts are...

Just thinking about this for a few seconds shows how unlikely it is to be true. Why on earth would a spider deliberately climb into someone's mouth? Spiders don't live in people's mouths. Even though they don't have very big brains, spiders can presumably tell that a mouth is not a comfortable resting place.

This entire story is a hoax. It was dreamed up and circulated (along with a bunch of other unbelievable stories) in 1993. Within months it had spread across the world by email, ending up being reported as fact in several newspapers.

Verdict : _____ **FICTION** _

> # Ferdinand Magellan was the first person ever to sail around the world.

The Portuguese explorer didn't set sail with the idea of travelling all around the world — he was actually trying to locate the Spice Islands in Indonesia. In 1519, Magellan left Spain to begin his momentous voyage. The five ships under his command sailed across the Atlantic but the journey became tough. Supplies were low and the crew began to starve. When they landed in the Philippines, disaster struck. Ferdinand Magellan became involved in a battle between local tribes — and was killed.

## ★ And the truth is...

The *Victoria* was the only one of the original five ships to circumnavigate the globe, but when it arrived back in Spain, Magellan wasn't on it. In fact, only 18 of the original crew were on board.

Verdict : _____ **FICTION** _

# Four fab things named after Magellan

Poor Magellan didn't make it all the way around the world, but he might have been pleased to know that after his untimely death a lot of stuff was named after him.

## 1. Magellanic penguin

Or, as experts (who love complicated words) like to call it, *Spheniscus magellanicus*. This beautiful penguin, which can be recognised by its stripes, lives in the…

## 2. …Strait of Magellan

This is a sea route that wriggles between the South American mainland and the archipelago of Tierra del Fuego. It's a great short cut and it was navigated by Magellan in 1520.

## 3. Magellan spacecraft

In 1989, this space probe became the very first to be launched from the Space Shuttle while it orbited Earth. Its mission was to map the surface of Venus. And it did.

## 4. Magellanic Clouds

They look like tiny clouds in the night sky, but they're not. The Magellanic Clouds are actual, true-life dwarf galaxies. And they too are named after Ferdinand Magellan.

F. Magellan

## No two snowflakes are the same

Snowflakes are one of the most basic and yet most beautiful objects in the natural world. In essence they are just ice crystals that fall from the clouds. A snowflake might be a single ice crystal or a collection of many ice crystals. However, they all have one thing in common; no matter how many crystals they are formed of they are all hexagonal, because that is the shape ice crystals are. So if all snowflakes are hexagonal does that mean they are all the same?

Imposter!

You're the imposter!

## ⭐ And the truth is...

The exact shape of a snowflake depends on lots of differing factors; how moist the air is or how cold it is for example. This can have a big effect on the shape. Each crystal will be hexagonal, but the variety within that basic outline can be staggering. There can be flakes with six long needle-like arms; or very flowery looking arms for instance. In fact the possibilities are literally endless — so no two snowflakes are ever exactly the same.

Verdict : _____ **FACT** _____

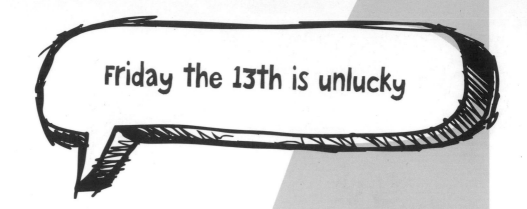

# Friday the 13th is unlucky

Fear that bad things will happen on Friday the 13th is so common among some people that it has even been given a name: *paraskevidekatriaphobia*. (Some sources say that once you can pronounce this, you're cured.)

This myth grew out of two separate ideas: firstly, that Fridays are unlucky, and secondly that anything to do with the number 13 is also terribly unlucky!

## 1 Fridays are unlucky

The idea that Friday is an unlucky day has been around for hundreds of years, since at least the 1600s. Although generally a bad day to do *anything*, there were some activities people said you should never, ever begin on a Friday:

 Launching a ship or boat for the first time, or starting a sea voyage (sailors have lots of superstitions!).

 Harvesting crops.

⭐ Getting married, giving birth (not that women have much choice about which day they do that), getting out of bed for the first time after being ill, or starting a new job.

## 2 Thirteen is an unlucky number

The idea that the number 13 is unlucky is sometimes said to come from ancient Norse myths. The legend goes that the goddess Frigga was banished to a mountaintop, where every Friday she would gather with 11 witches and the Devil — making 13 of them in total.

Other people claim that the source of the myth is numerology, the ancient study of the mystical significance of numbers. According to numerology, 12 was thought of as a 'complete' number, because there were 12 months of the year, 12 signs of the zodiac, 12 hours on a clock, 12 apostles of Jesus, etc. Adding one to make 13 creates a bad number.

## ★ And the truth is...

In any large group of people, there's bound to be someone who can tell you about someone else who had terrible things happen to them on Friday 13th. Of course, terrible things also happen on Wednesday 22nd, Sunday 3rd, Thursday 25th, etc, etc. But no one asks about that, or remembers it!

Verdict : —— FICTION ——

# ⭐ 5 things you (probably) didn't know about DOGS

**1** The tallest dog ever is a Great Dane who is 112 cm high at the shoulder.

**2** The smallest recorded dog was a 6.35 cm Yorkshire terrier.

**3** Louis Doberman, a German tax collector, developed the Doberman breed. He wanted fierce, strong dogs to protect him while he collected money from people!

**4** When their dog died, grief-stricken ancient Egyptians are said to have shaved off their own eyebrows and smeared their hair with mud.

**5** A dog's nose print is as unique as a human fingerprint.

# When animals ATTACK!

## Escaping a gorilla

There you are, wandering through the African highlands one day. Suddenly, you come face to face with a giant male silverback gorilla — and he's not very happy to have been woken from his favourite afternoon nap.

If he starts hooting, then throwing plants (and possibly a bit of his own poo) at you, he's going into attack mode.

How do you avoid being torn limb from limb?

⭐ Don't look him in the eye — instead, look down at the ground and to one side.

⭐ Slowly back away, but without turning around until you can no longer see the grumpy giant.

⭐ If he does attack, your best hope — and it's not a very good one, to be honest — is to curl up into a ball and 'play dead'!

You can go around the world in a hot-air balloon in 80 days!

In the 19th century, Phileas Fogg the Victorian adventurer set off on an amazing voyage, to travel around the world in 80 days by rail, steamer, elephant and sledge*, and arriving back in London just before the deadline to claim his reward.

All good so far, except ... Phileas Fogg wasn't real. He's pure fiction — a character invented by French sci-fi author Jules Verne, whose book *Around the World in Eighty Days* became a bestseller when it was published in 1873.

So if it doesn't take 80 days, how long *does* it take to travel around the world?

## ★ And the truth is...

In 1870, US businessman George Francis Train travelled around the globe in 80 days. It's very likely that Jules Verne read about this in the newspaper. And in 1872, he may also have seen an advert for travel agent Thomas Cook's more leisurely round-the-world trip that lasted about seven months — and presumably also allowed travellers a little time to sightsee along the way. So Verne knew the journey could be done in 80 days and he also knew that people were growing more interested in world travel. If he were still alive, he'd also know that it's now possible to fly around the world in a passenger jet in just over two days.

* But not balloon, which is the mode of transport most usually associated with Fogg.

Verdict : FICTION

## In space nobody can hear you scream

Sound is amazing. It can travel huge distances and amazing speeds, but sometimes you won't hear even the loudest noises. For example, elephants make a sound that can travel for miles, but this is nothing compared to the noises whales make. These whale songs can travel hundreds of kilometres — but we don't hear them because whales and elephants make sounds we can't hear. But a scream we can hear, so surely we should be able to hear one in the quiet of deep space.

## ⭐ And the truth is...

Sound travels at around 1,225 km/h (761 mph) through the air. But even more astounding is the fact that it travels four times quicker through water than through air. That's because sound needs molecules to travel. The molecules vibrate against each other and that's how noise moves. The molecules are closer together in water than in air, so sound goes faster. However in space there are no molecules so sound doesn't travel at all. And no travel means no noise — you can scream as loud as you want, but nobody is going to hear you.

Verdict :  FACT

# A sneeze is more deadly than a bullet

A bullet is an effective way of killing or injuring someone. It needs a charge of exploding gunpowder to provide the force to send it flying through the air. If it hits someone, things get very messy indeed. A sneeze on the other hand is a reaction to something irritating your nose. It's easy to see which one is more dangerous.

Arghhh!

## And the truth is...

Perhaps it's not quite so clear after all. A sneeze is also a very effective way of spreading germs, and germs can be exceedingly dangerous. In 1918 World War I finished claiming the lives of up to 17 million people. The same year there was an outbreak of Spanish flu. It spread across much of the world killing an estimated 50 million people. So the flu killed more than a world war — better get your tissues ready.

Verdict : **FACT** and **FICTION**

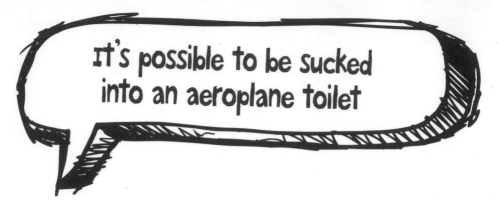

# It's possible to be sucked into an aeroplane toilet

*'I heard of a woman on an Air France flight who pushed the flush button accidentally, and her bottom was sucked down into the toilet. She was so stuck that firemen had to free her when the flight landed.'*

This is a brilliant example of an urban myth, which usually happens to someone else. And aeroplane toilets certainly do flush very strongly, as anyone who's heard the *WHOOSH!* of air as they go off will agree.

## ⭐ And the truth is...

The suction created by an aeroplane toilet flushing is not strong enough to wedge a person into the bowl. Plus, all toilets have a little gap at the front and space between the seat and the top of the toilet bowl. This would make it impossible for anyone to get sealed onto the seat.

Verdict :  **FICTION**

## You're taller in the morning than in the evening

Imagine you want to join the army. But there's a minimum height requirement: you have to be 173 cm (5 ft, 8ins) tall. You get a friend to measure you and — disaster — you're 2 cm (roughly half an inch) short! Then the friend says, hang on, we'll measure you again in the morning. Everyone knows we're all taller first thing in the morning: you'll be the right height then.

Could it work?

## ⭐ And the truth is...

All through the day, gravity acts on our bodies. It squishes down our knee joints and our spines, slowly forcing the bones closer together. Each joint is only affected a tiny bit, but they all add up. When we lie down to go to sleep again, the joints return to their natural position, a little bit further apart. So you are taller in the morning than the evening, by about 2 cm.

Verdict : ———————  FACT

## Ostriches bury their heads in the sand

The full version of this is that when scared or threatened, ostriches will quickly bury their heads in the sand. It's a birdy version of what little kids sometimes do; they cover their eyes with their hands and shout:

*'You can't see me!'*

If it's true, it proves that ostriches are remarkably stupid, and makes you wonder how on earth they've managed to survive for so long.

## ★ And the truth is...

Ostriches do put their heads in holes in the sand — but not because they're scared. They dig holes in the dirt to lay their eggs, and regularly lean down into the hole to turn the eggs with their beaks. From a distance, it can look as though they're burying their heads in the sand.

Verdict : **FICTION**

# Touching a toad gives you warts

When you think of witches do you think of bubbling cauldrons? Black cats and broomsticks? Toads hopping and leaping everywhere? Warty noses?

Maybe it's this image of warty witches that gives us the idea that touching a toad will give you warts. Or maybe it's the way toads look. Their skin is often covered in lumps and bumps that look like warts. Since the toads are covered in warty growths, and warts are infectious, it's obvious that if you touch a toad you'll get warts. Isn't it..?

## And the truth is...

Toads aren't covered in warts. The lumps on their skin are glands, which release mucus or poison when the toad is alarmed or threatened.

We get warts from a virus, called HPV. The H stands for 'human' — showing that the virus is a human one... not a toad one.

Verdict :  **FICTION**

# Loos in History

### The Garderobe
This was a medieval toilet in a castle — a tiny room in which there was a hole. This led not to sewers, but straight out into the fresh air. Waste simply fell through the hole and dribbled down the outside of the castle wall. Ewww.

## The Common Jakes
This was the name of Henry VIII's massive 28-seater toilet at Hampton Court. Of course, he didn't use it himself. Instead, the king used...

## The Closed Stool
Henry VIII had a particularly beautiful toilet, with a padded seat for his royal bottom. It was decorated with so many gilt nails that it must have looked golden. It didn't flush, but that was OK because kings and queens employed someone else to empty their toilet for them.

## The Outside Loo
Even during the last century, which isn't that long ago, many people used an outside loo, which was usually in their back yard. But it got pretty cold in winter, which is why (particularly at night-time) many preferred to use...

## A Chamber Pot
This was a container that went under the bed — a sort of mini portable toilet. There was no flush, of course. So by the morning, it could get very smelly.

# One side of the Moon is permanently dark

You hear expressions like 'moonshine' and it makes it sound like the Moon provides its own light, like the Sun. It doesn't — we see the Moon because it is lit up by the Sun. But what do we see?

If you look at the Moon you always see the same side. The Moon might wax and wane — go to a full then to a crescent shape — but it's always the same bit of it we see. We never get to see the other side. This has led many people to suggest that the Moon doesn't rotate and therefore there is a 'dark side' of the Moon that never gets lit up by the Sun.

## ⭐ And the truth is...

Those people are wrong on both counts. The Moon does rotate, it's just that its rotation roughly coincides with Earth's, so we always see the same face. Secondly, as the Moon orbits around the Sun, all of its faces see the light of the Sun. When we see the new Moon — when it looks like the Moon is barely there at all — is when the Moon is between us and the Sun. Then what we think of as the 'dark side' of the Moon is actually getting the Sun's light.

Verdict :

**FICTION**

# It'll NEVER WORK!

'The horse is here to stay, but the automobile is only a novelty, a fad.'

A banker explaining why it would be a bad idea to invest in the Ford Motor company, 1903.

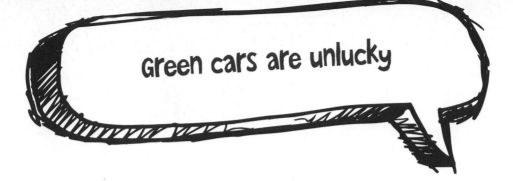

# Green cars are unlucky

It's said that people learning to drive will often refuse to take lessons in a green car, because they think it's an unlucky colour and it will be impossible to pass their test. Racing drivers apparently hate competing in green cars, because it's impossible to win in one, and they're more likely to crash.

In fact, it's not only cars: green boats are said to be unlucky. It's also claimed to be very bad luck to wear green at a wedding. Actors also think that green is an unlucky colour (mind you, actors have almost as many superstitions as sailors).

 ## And the truth is...

This myth may have grown out of early racing accidents involving green cars. In 1911, 11 people were killed in Syracuse, USA, when a green race car crashed. Then in 1920, famous driver Gaston Chevrolet died after a green car hit his own. But no statistics show that green cars are more likely to crash, or are unlucky in any other way.

Though green is considered unlucky in the UK, USA and Canada, in other places, such as Islamic countries, green is thought to be the colour of paradise!

Verdict :  **FICTION**

# ATTACK!

## Escaping a crocodile

It's a beautiful warm evening, you're on holiday — why not take a walk down by that tropical river? **BECAUSE IT'S FULL OF CROCODILES!**

Here's how to avoid becoming a croco-dinner:

 *Don't swim or wade in areas where crocodiles are found. Sounds obvious, but each year many people are killed by crocs while doing just that.*

*Crocodiles are rubbish at running from side to side, so if one chases you, run in zig-zags.*

*Stay away from the water's edge, and always face the water – they wait till your back's turned to attack.*

*Don't visit the same spot day after day – one day, there will be a croc waiting for you.*

## You can hypnotise an alligator

This story goes that if you know what you're doing, you can put an alligator into a hypnotic trance. This renders it helpless and unable to move.

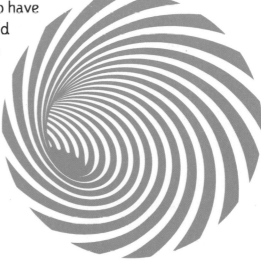

Florida's Seminole Indians are said to have discovered this trick. They would hold the alligator's mouth shut — which is easy, because they have very weak jaw-opening muscles. Then they would roll the alligator on its back with its tail held still, and its belly was stroked. The alligator would go into a trance, and would only wake up when someone touched it.

### ★ And the truth is...

This can be done, and not only on alligators. Some sharks have been put into a similar trance-like state, for example. (Don't try and fight off a shark attack by tickling its tummy, though...)

Verdict :

## The Aztecs loved bungee jumping!

Bungee jumping is not for the faint-hearted*. Fans of this extreme sport launch themselves from bridges, cranes and sometimes helicopters, with their feet tied to a long elastic cord. They fall … and then *boing* upwards … and then fall again. This goes on until there is no bounce left in the cord.

So how did the Aztecs have the technology to make an elastic cord made of multiple strands of elastic and covered with polypropylene? They must have been light years ahead of other ancient peoples when it came to science.

### ★ And the truth is...

The Aztecs *did* bungee jump! But for them, it was a ceremony, not an extreme sport. In the Flying Men Dance, five brave souls climb to the top of a 30-metre pole and then four jump into the air (on the end of ropes). The fifth stands atop the pole and plays musical instruments as the pole slowly rotates, lowering the four flyers to the ground. It's much slower and more tuneful than modern bungee jumping. And amazingly, it's still done today.

Verdict : _____ **FICTION** _____

Queen Victoria wore black
for 39 years

When Alexandrina Victoria became queen in 1837, she was just 18 years old. Two years later, she married her sweetheart — and her cousin — Prince Albert, who became the Prince Consort. They had a very happy marriage and nine children. But in December 1861, tragedy struck when the Prince Consort died. Queen Victoria was totally grief-stricken. In keeping with tradition, she immediately put away all of her grand, colourful dresses *forever*. And then she began to wear black.

 **And the truth is...**

Queen Victoria went on wearing black — and on and on. In fact, so sad was she about Albert's death that she wore black until she herself died in January 1901.

Verdict :

# There is no gravity in space

Gravity is the force that keeps us on the ground and stops us from floating off into space. There's gravity on the Moon too; but as the Moon is only one sixth the size of the Earth its gravity is only as sixth as strong. That's why astronauts could bounce around the surface like they did.

## ⭐ And the truth is...

The further away from the Earth you get the weaker the pull of gravity is. So, astronauts in space can float around inside their spacecraft. However that doesn't mean there is no gravity there — on the contrary there's loads of it. For example it's the Earth's gravity that keeps the Moon orbiting around us. It's the Sun's gravity that keeps all the planets orbiting around it. Without it we could be literally anywhere.

Verdict : **FICTION**

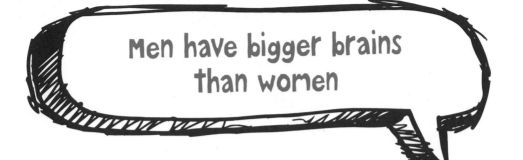

# Men have bigger brains than women

Who's better — boys or girls? It's an argument that's been going for years and years and years; and will keep going as long as there are still boys and girls on the planet. One of the big arguments is who is more intelligent — who's got the biggest brains?

Studies show that when babies are born, baby boys tend to have bigger brains. However they also tend to be bigger overall — girls born the same size have exactly the same size brain. Yet as we grow up men's brains tend to be around 10% bigger than women's. But does this mean men are more intelligent? No, as studies also show that men simply have bigger heads. Besides, it's not how big your brain that matters — it's how you use it that counts.

Verdict :  but so what?

117

'At least it'll be a clean bite. Won't it?'

## A dog's bite is cleaner than a human's

People will tell you that, if you have a choice between being bitten by a human or by a dog, you should pick the dog. (People who give you this advice always seem to forget that dogs are MUCH better at biting than humans — but let's leave that aside for now.) The dog's mouth is cleaner, they say, so there's less chance of the bite getting infected...

## ★ And the truth is...

You don't have to think about this for very long to realise it may not be true. Dogs use their mouths for everything, including picking up dead rats, licking their toilet parts, eating and biting. Their mouths *can't* be as clean as someone who brushes their teeth and only uses their mouth for eating, talking and kissing! BUT, the things that make a bite likely to become infected are bacteria. Bacteria are mostly species-specific, so dog bacteria are harmful to dogs, human bacteria to humans. If a dog bites you, it delivers dog bacteria into the wound. This is less likely to be harmful. It doesn't mean a dog's bite is cleaner — just that it comes with the 'right' kind of dirt.

Verdict : _____ nearly FACT _____

# Where In The World?

Wowzer! This gravy packs a punch!

**You would assume that the delicious curry dish chicken tikka masala was invented in India, right?**

Wrong. In the 1970s, when a man in an Indian restaurant in the Scottish city of Glasgow asked for gravy with his meat, the chef didn't know what gravy was, and so mixed together tomato soup, spices and yoghurt. Chicken tikka masala was born.

Today, chicken tikka masala is often said to be the most popular meal in Britain. It even rivals fish and chips as the country's national dish.

# I'd never have known...

**Well, perhaps that's a bit of an exaggeration. But donkeys are the only animals of their size that will face up to a lion, rather than running away.**

That's why in Africa, brave (if a bit daft) donkeys are sometimes used to guard herds of cattle against attacks by lions.

# 5 things you (probably) didn't know about CATS

**1** Cats can squeeze through any space wide enough for their whiskers.

**2** Only cats, giraffes and camels walk using both left legs, then both right legs.

**3** Cats can make ten times as many noises as dogs.

**4** Strangely, cats are unable to taste sweet food.

**5** If you put a cat on a vegetarian diet, it will die.

# Lewis Carroll's 'Mad Hatter' is based on fact

The Mad Hatter from *Alice's Adventures in Wonderland* is totally, definitely 100% mad. But did Lewis Carroll — who wrote the book — base his character on real hatters? They can't all have been mad, surely?

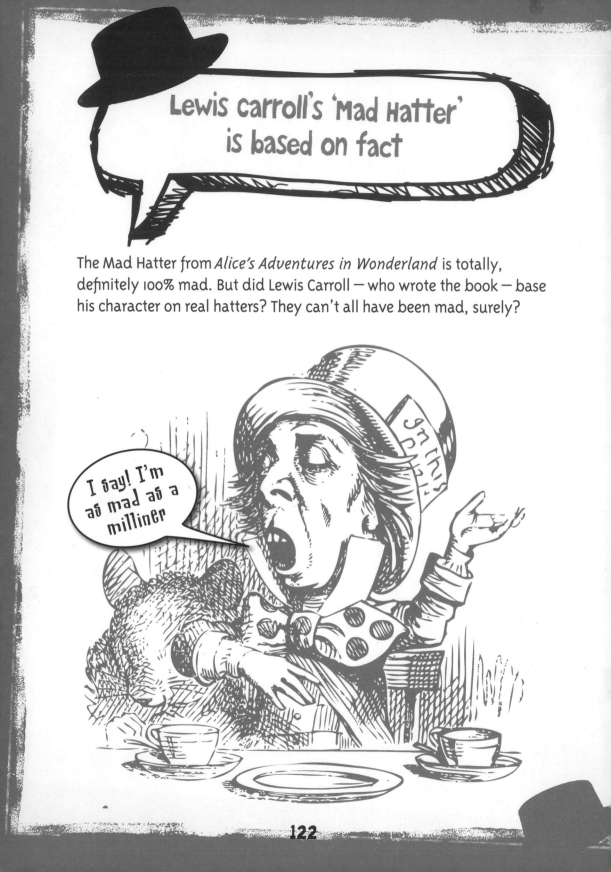

I say! I'm as mad as a milliner

## ⭐ And the truth is…

A hatter is someone who makes hats, who is also known as a milliner. In the past, a lot of hats were made from felt — a type of woollen material. Instead of being woven like other fabrics, felt is pressed and matted. But in the 18th and 19th centuries, another ingredient was used in the felt-making process. And that was mercury.

Mercury — also known as quicksilver — is used in thermometers, barometers and many other devices. It's a very useful chemical, but it's a very poisonous one too. Sadly, in the 18th and 19th centuries, no one knew this. After breathing in mercury fumes day after day, workers in hat factories were unaware that they were v-e-r-y s-l-o-w-l-y being poisoned.

The symptoms of mercury poisoning include impaired sight and vision, tingling or numb skin, depression, tremors and hallucinations*. But doctors didn't realise that mercury was to blame and simply thought that the hatters had gone mad.

Verdict :  FACT (a bit)

\* Seeing things that aren't actually there.

123

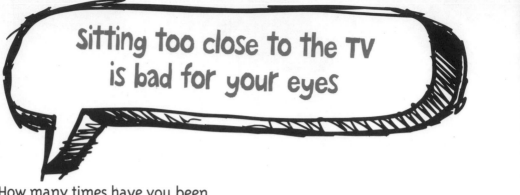

# sitting too close to the TV is bad for your eyes

How many times have you been told that you shouldn't sit too close to the television? It'll ruin your eyesight. You'll get square eyes. You'll turn into a lazy, bloated, couch potato. It's been the same message since television first started to become popular in the 1950s.

## ★ And the truth is...

Televisions produce radiation — and too much radiation can be bad for you. Back in the 1950s no one really understood how harmful the radiation coming from televisions could be and watching too much TV caused some people eye problems such as myopia, or short-sightedness as it is more commonly known. Nowadays televisions shield viewers from radiation, so sitting too close won't harm you. Mind you, watch too much television and you might get eye-strain; and you'll definitely turn into a couch potato.

Verdict : Mainly  FICTION

# BIG FILMS BAD SCIENCE

## Time Travelling Travesties

The idea of time travel has interested scientists and movie-makers alike, but thinking about it and how it would really work makes your head hurt.

1. **The present as you know it wouldn't exist.** Any changes in the past would alter the chain of events that led to everything being where it was in the future.

2. **An alternate Universe would be formed alongside the original.** The alternate Universe would be like the original Universe, but changed from the moment the time travellers arrived.

In the *Back to the Future* films (where a scientist makes a time machine from an old sports car) both of these things happen, which it can't as it's either one or the other. But the biggest problem with time travel into the past is that it's not possible. You would have to travel faster than light to do so, and top scientist Albert Einstein tells us that nothing travels faster than light — not even an old sports car or a Tardis.

# You can tell someone's character from how they look

There are lots of myths about how you can tell what a person is like from their appearance. Just apply a few simple rules based on well-known guidelines and, hey presto! You'll know exactly what kind of person you're dealing with.

Here are just a few of the most popular myths:

### 'Never trust someone whose eyes are too close together'

Such people are often described as having 'shifty' eyes. Other myths associated with eyes are that if the eyes slope upward the person will be an opportunist; if you can see the whites of someone's eyes above their iris, they have a terrible temper; and if the eyes slope downward, that person will be eager to please everyone.

### 'A weak chin shows lack of determination'

Chins are said to be a reliable way of forecasting someone's character. The 'weak chin = lack of determination' myth is very common, but chins are the source of lots of other myths. For

example, people expect a man with a jutting jaw to be aggressive. It's often said that you should never trust a man with a beard — presumably because for some sinister reason he's hiding his chin.

### 'People with low brows lack intelligence/are more likely to be criminals'

A low brow — especially when combined with a short forehead, low hairline and eyebrows that meet in the middle — is often said to show someone is unintelligent, aggressive, quick-tempered and jealous.

 ### And the truth is...

There's no evidence that the way people look has ANY link to how they behave. What happens is that we've already heard, for example, that someone with a jutting jaw will be aggressive. So when we meet someone with a jutting jaw, we pay special attention to behaviour that fits our idea of them.

Verdict :___ **FICTION** ___

## All dogs have a bit of wolf in them

It's easy to believe that an Alsatian or a husky might be descended from wolves. But a Yorkshire terrier, or a Chihuahua? No way... surely not?

 ## The truth is...

Incredibly, all dogs are descended from wolves — even Paris Hilton's Tinkerbell. No one knows how humans and wolves first got together. Maybe wolves started nosing around humans and got less and less nervous of them. Or maybe humans found some wolf cubs and decided to adopt them.

So, why don't all dogs look like wolves? It's because over the centuries (dogs have been alongside us for about 13,000 years), we've bred them for specific uses. For example, you wouldn't send a greyhound to catch rats, or a Jack Russell to run around a track.

Verdict : **FACT**

Hyenas are so nasty, they laugh when they've killed something

Most people who have seen hyenas instinctively fear them. They look like a kind of Frankenstein's dog. With their snarling faces, sloped backs and powerful shoulders they look like a cross between a cat and a wolf. And you're right to be scared. A quarter of all animals that are hunted as prey in Africa are killed by hyenas.

Hyenas are extremely aggressive. They're usually born as twins, but one twin often eats the other to show it who's boss (which certainly works). As adults, they can eat a third of their bodyweight in just half an hour.

Worst of all, hyenas are said to laugh as they eat into their victims (often before they're even dead).

 **And the truth is...**

Hyenas do laugh at a kill site — but not for joy. What sounds to us like a laugh is actually a weaker member of the hyena pack showing submission to a stronger one. He or she is saying, 'Don't bite me — you eat first. I'll just wait till you've finished.'

Verdict : _____

FACT

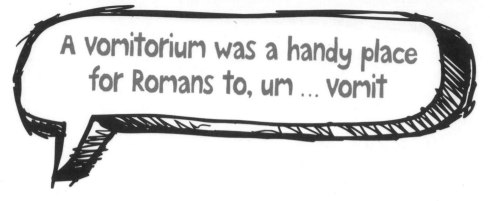

A vomitorium was a handy place for Romans to, um ... vomit

*Bleurgh*. It's enough to make your stomach churn. Centuries ago, rich Romans gorged themselves on dubious delicacies such as songbirds, ostrich brains and sows' udders, until they were fit to burst. But then, it's said that instead of pushing away their plates and saying, 'Goodness, I'm full,' the Romans simply popped along to the vomitorium. There, they could be spectacularly sick in private, before going back to the dining room and continuing with their feast. Or so the story goes…

## ⭐ And the truth is...

Romans headed for the vomitorium *not* when they were feeling a bit green, but when they wanted to make a swift exit. Vomitoria — the word for more than one vomitorium — were nothing to do with vomiting. They were actually passages designed to allow the speedy, efficient emptying of an amphitheatre after a performance.

Verdict :  **FICTION**

# Cleopatra had a beard

Cleopatra VII (69–30BC) was the last pharaoh of Ancient Egypt, famous for her beauty, her men (Julius Caesar and Mark Antony), and her suicide by asp-bite*. Shakespeare wrote a play about her; Hollywood made films about her. But did one of ancient history's most beautiful women really have a beard?

## ⭐ And the truth is...

In Ancient Egypt, it was traditional for pharaohs to wear a false beard as a symbol of their power. Tutankhamun's death mask had a very ornate, very long beard. And it wasn't just the male pharaohs that wore them. Ancient statues of Hatshepsut, another female pharaoh, show her wearing a beard too. So Cleopatra probably *did* have a beard, but it would have been fake and she would only have worn it on special occasions, to show who was in charge.

* See pages 170–171.

Verdict : _____

# A tomato is really a fruit

We all know the difference between fruit and vegetables. Fruit is the healthy stuff you can eat for snacks and/or dessert. Vegetables are the healthy things that come on your plate next to the meat or fish. Or if you're a vegetarian it's the stuff that comes on your plate. And if you're a vegetarian you should really know the difference. And just to prove to yourself that you know which is which take this simple quiz:

**Decide whether the following foods are either fruits or vegetables:**

**(a) Tomato**

**(b) Orange**

**(c) Cabbage**

**(d) Onion**

**(e) Pumpkin**

**(f) Turnip**

**(g) Leek**

**(h) Apple**

**(i) Banana**

**(j) Potato**

**(k) Peas**

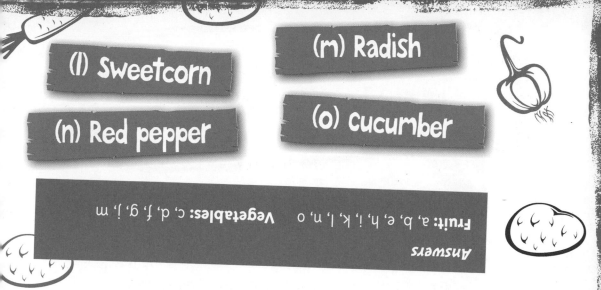

**(l) Sweetcorn**

**(m) Radish**

**(n) Red pepper**

**(o) Cucumber**

A simple way of telling the difference between the two is that fruit have seeds and vegetables don't. Peas and sweetcorn are actually seeds, and that's why they are fruit. This also means that nuts technically are fruit; as are cereals like wheat and other grains.

Of course how we use these various fruits and vegetables is what is really important. As the famous quote puts it:

*'Knowledge is knowing a tomato is a fruit; wisdom is knowing not to put it in a fruit salad.'*

We don't know who said it, but they got it spot on.

## ★ And the truth is...

Surprisingly a tomato is a fruit, and so are many things you might have thought were vegetables. Have a look at the answers to the quiz and see.

Verdict : _____

**FACT**

133

# A scuba diver was once mistakenly dumped onto a forest fire

You know those planes that scoop up a bellyful of water from a lake, then fly over a forest fire and offload it? Well, this myth tells of a scuba diver who was out diving not far below the surface, when he heard a strange, loud rumbling.

The story goes that a split-second later, the diver was whisked out of the lake, along with the water he'd been swimming in, and into the belly of a fire-fighting plane. The plane flew on for a few minutes, then spilled out the water, scuba diver and all, onto a forest fire!

## ★ And the truth is...

There are versions of this story from the western USA, Australia, Greece... just about anywhere that has forest fires. The only problem with it is, it's not true. Planes do scoop up water for fire fighting, but there's no evidence one of them has ever scooped up a diver as well. Phew!

Verdict : **FICTION**

## Eskimos kiss by rubbing noses

The full version of this myth is that the Inuit live in such a cold place that they dare not kiss each other on the lips. If they did, their lips might freeze together — making it less a kiss than a marathon snog, at least until they could get somewhere warm enough to get unglued. So instead, they rub noses in a greeting they call the 'Eskimo kiss'.

## ★ And the truth is...

The Inuit do greet their closest friends and family using their noses. They place their upper lip and nose against the other person's skin and breathe in. But this is not a kiss, and has nothing to do with the danger of lips getting frozen together. It's just a different form of greeting.

Verdict : ___ **FICTION** ___

# ⭐ 5 things you (probably) didn't know about SHARKS

**1** There are no known diseases that affect sharks.

**2** Sharks can carry on biting even if their own insides have been bitten out.

**3** Sharks won't eat near the place where they've given birth ...

**4** ... but they will eat *anything*, anywhere else.

**5** Bull sharks – which regularly attack humans – can swim in both sea and fresh water.

Just a few of the things found in the stomachs of sharks: ★ a tom-tom drum ★ a chicken coop ★ a pair of shoes ★ a chair ★ an unexploded bomb.

# I'd never have known...

## ... that walruses are right-handed

**Walruses just love to eat clams, which live buried in the seabed. They like them so much that a walrus can pack away over 6,000 juicy clams in one meal.**

To expose the clams, walruses fan away the surrounding material using their front flipper. And they almost always use the right flipper to do this, very rarely the left.

> # In the Middle Ages, everyone thought the world was flat.

It is said that the famous explorer Christopher Columbus struggled to win approval for his first voyage in 1492 because people believed the world was flat — and that he would simply sail off the end of it. Splosh!

## ★ And the truth is...

A *very* long time ago many people *did* think that our planet was flat. But as early as the 6th century BC, the Greek mathematician Pythagoras had begun to suspect that Earth was spherical. The idea caught on. And by the time that Columbus was thinking of sailing across the Atlantic Ocean, most people knew that the world was round.

Verdict :  **FICTION**

## Did you know...?

Amazingly, despite all evidence to the contrary (including photos taken by spacecraft orbiting around our planet) some people still think that Earth is flat. They belong to the Flat Earth Society. Presumably, they have never been on a world cruise.

Earth is an oblate spheroid, which means that it's like a slightly flattened ball. So it might not be a perfect sphere, but it's definitely not flat.

# Your IQ stays fixed throughout your life

Your IQ — or Intelligence Quotient to give it its full name — is a rough measure of your intelligence. Scientists measure your IQ by taking your mental age (which they get from a series of tests) and dividing it by your actual age and then multiplying the number by 100. The final figure is your IQ — a score of 100 is said to be average.

Obviously people know a lot more when they are 20 years old as compared to when they were 5 years old, so obviously their IQ has gone up. Or has it?

## ★ And the truth is...

IQ tests are adjusted for age. After you reach 16 the idea of a 'mental age' is abandoned and instead your test results are compared to what is considered to be the average score for your age. So, although you might know more stuff your IQ score would stay roughly the same throughout your life.

Verdict :

# BIG FILMS BAD SCIENCE

## Back from the Dead

Mary Shelley wrote *Frankenstein* in the early 1800s and it has been made into countless films. The story is of a mad scientist (scientists in films are always mad) called Dr Frankenstein who stitches together various bits of dead bodies and brings his creation to life using electricity.

Shelley might well have been inspired by the work of Luigi Galvani. This Italian scientist noticed that electricity made the legs of a dead frog move, concluding that electricity was a vital part of life. His experiments were groundbreaking.

They were also wrong. A modern-day defibrillator might get a heart working again, but it takes more than electricity for life. Even if Dr Frankenstein could have connected all the veins and arteries together, there would be too much decay, blood loss and tissue damage for his creation ever to live — never mind move.

## You can unlock a car using a mobile phone

This is one of many myths about things you can do with a mobile phone, from cooking eggs (see page 39) to blowing up petrol stations (see page 167).

*It goes like this:* If you lose your car keys while you're out, don't panic. All you need to do is call home, then ask someone there to get the key. Have them point the 'blipper' at the phone, and point *your* phone at the car. The signal will be transmitted between the phones and to the car, which will unlock.

## ★ And the truth is...

There are a couple of problems with this myth. First of all, it doesn't work. Mobile phones transmit sound that humans can hear, but a car's automatic locking system uses a radio frequency we can't hear. Because they use different frequencies, the phone *can't* unlock the car.

The other problem is that even if you could unlock the car, you wouldn't be able to drive it — you still don't have the key. What you *would* have is an unlocked car, which you're about to abandon while you fetch the key.

Verdict : _____  _____

## cow farts are destroying the world

This myth is all about global warming. Global warming is caused by an increase in the number of greenhouse gases in the atmosphere. These gases trap heat, slowly increasing the world's temperature. This is causing all kinds of trouble: changes in our weather, a rise in sea levels, and an increase in natural disasters such as hurricanes.

But what's all that got to do with cows?

There are millions and millions of cows in the world, and they're constantly eating, which produces a lot of wee, poo and farts. Unfortunately, cow farts contain the greenhouse gas methane — which is far worse for the environment than the most common greenhouse gas, carbon dioxide.

## ★ And the truth is...

Cow farts aren't destroying the world. It's their burps. They burp out loads of methane every day — some estimates say they constitute 4% of the world's greenhouse gas emissions! And because methane is so much more damaging than carbon dioxide, cow burps are having a really big effect.

Verdict : ___ the right idea, but actually **FICTION**

# ⭐ 5 things you (probably) didn't know about ELEPHANTS

**1** Elephants are the only mammals that can't jump, but ...

**2** ... they *can* stand on their heads – which only elephants and humans can do.

**3** Elephants only sleep for two hours a day.

**4** Elephants can't run, as it would damage their bones. Mind you, they can do a fast walk of 25 kph.

**5** Up to nine litres of water can be held inside an elephant's trunk.

# TOOTH TRUTHS

1. The very first false teeth date back to northern Italy in 700BC. They were made from old human or animal teeth, held together by gold wire.

2. Sir Winston Churchill's false teeth were sold for a small fortune at auction in 2011. Well, they did belong to a very famous wartime prime minister. (And they were made of gold.)

3. Archaeologists have found ancient false teeth in Mexico, made from wolf teeth. They must have been a howling success.

4. After the Battle of Waterloo in 1815, people plucked teeth from dead – and sometimes not-quite-dead – soldiers and sold them to dentists. They were extremely popular and became known as Waterloo Teeth.

5. The Japanese invented wooden false teeth.

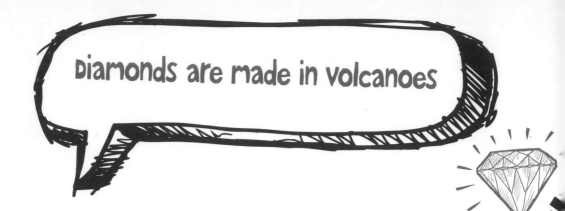

## Diamonds are made in volcanoes

According to a famous old song, diamonds are a girl's best friend. Now the girl's living, breathing, human best friend might take exception to that, but we can kind of see what the song is saying: diamonds are so precious and valuable anyone would want one.

Diamonds are basically just lumps of tightly pressed carbon, but when cut and polished are uniquely beautiful. Because of this diamonds have been prized throughout history and have often been used in jewellery, as they are today. One of the biggest diamonds ever found, named the Cullinan, can be found in the crown jewels of the British Royal Family.

Diamonds are also the hardest natural substance on Earth. It is used in industry for lots of different jobs, such as cutting other materials, or grinding substances down.

But how is such a useful substance made? Many people think diamonds can occur in coal seams, as coal is basically compressed carbon, too.

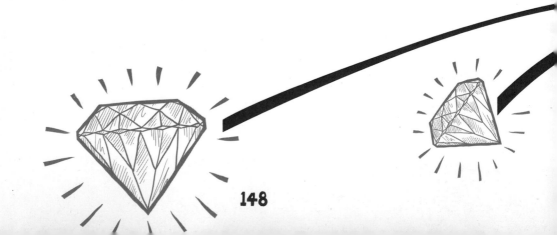

# ⭐ And the truth is...

Diamonds are much older than the first plants, and as coal is fossilized plant matter then that rules that idea out. For diamonds to form there needs to be extreme pressure and extreme heat — around 1050 °C (1922 °F) would do it — and the only place to find that combination is in the Earth's mantle, which lies below the Earth's surface layer.

And the only way for diamonds to get from the mantle to the surface is to hitch a ride on a volcanic eruption.

Verdict : _____ **FACT** _____

# A penguin was once stolen from a zoo!

This urban myth was very popular a few years ago. The story went that a 12-year-old boy became fascinated by the penguins at Boston Zoo. (Lots of urban myths have specific locations like this — it makes them more believable.)

In fact, the boy became so fascinated that he decided to take a penguin away with him. He popped one in his backpack, and went home.

The theft was only discovered when his mother went to investigate strange noises in the bathroom, and discovered her son sitting at one end of the bath… and a penguin at the other.

## ★ And the truth is...

It's a great story, but Boston Zoo counted all their penguins when this tall tale first appeared: none were missing. They also pointed out that versions of this story set in other zoos have appeared before.

Verdict : **FICTION**

# You can drink your own wee to survive

Imagine the scene: you're out for a hike in the remote mountains. Disaster strikes! You slip and fall, breaking your leg. The hot sun beats down, so you take a drink from your water bottle. Help will come soon.

The next day, still no one has come. Your throat is dry and sore, your water is all gone. You remember hearing somewhere that it's possible to drink your own wee to survive. Revolting — but can it be true?

## ★ The answer is...

This is 100% true — and if it's a choice between drinking your own wee and dying, the wee might not seem so revolting after all. Wee is about 95% water, and the rest of it is made up of things that would not normally do you any harm.

Some people even claim drinking wee is good for you. They put it in the fridge overnight, then drink it instead of orange juice at breakfast. Erm, bottoms up!

Verdict : _____

# POLAR NOSES

Polar bears are just about perfectly designed for hunting seals out on the Arctic ice. They're the largest land-based meat eater, and are armed with some pretty terrifying weapons:

 *Huge feet up to 30 cm across, support the bear's weight as it stalks its prey across the snow and ice. They are tipped with claws that can rip a seal's belly open.*

 *An amazing sense of smell, which allows the bear to smell seals from 1.5 km away, and through a metre of snow.*

 *A top speed of 40 kph.*

 *Powerful jaws that can crush a seal's skull in one bite.*

There's just one problem for the polar bear. Its white coat is ideal camouflage for creeping up on seals — but its black nose isn't. That nose stands out like a cherry in the middle of a white-iced cake. So as the bears creep up on their prey, they apparently cover their noses with their paws.

# BEARS COVER THEIR WHEN HUNTING

**And the truth is...**

The idea of polar bears covering their black noses for better disguise is often repeated. It appears in the myths of some Arctic native peoples, who use it to show what a careful and dangerous hunter the bear is. But despite the fact that many polar bears have their own film-crew entourages, no one has ever recorded a polar bear doing this.

Verdict : **FICTION**

A few more (untrue) myths about polar bears:

1. All polar bears are left-handed.

2. Polar bears use tools to kill their prey (for example by throwing blocks of ice at them).

3. The only animal that hunts polar bears is the killer whale (actually, polar bears are a top predator: nothing hunts them except humans).

Marie Antoinette said,
'Let them eat cake.'

When Marie Antoinette, the rich wife of Louis XVI of 18th century France, was told that the peasants didn't have enough bread, it's said that she replied, 'Let them eat cake.' How rude!

## ★ And the truth is...

What Marie Antoinette is actually supposed to have said is, *'Qu'ils mangent de la brioche.'* Brioche is not cake, but a delicious type of bread made with lots of eggs and butter. In the 18th century, there was a French law that declared that if bakers ran out of ordinary bread, they had to sell the more expensive brioche at the same low price as the bread. This was to make sure that they made enough of the cheap bread to go round. So Marie Antoinette may have just been saying that if the bakers had run out of cheap bread, then the French peasants should just buy cheap brioche instead.

But it is doubtful whether Marie Antoinette mentioned brioche at all. The phrase was way older than the queen herself. And as the French had seriously fallen out of love with their royal family, it's unlikely she would have tried to annoy them further with silly suggestions about cake or bread. In fact, the heads of Marie Antoinette and Louis XVI were sliced off by the guillotine in 1793.

Verdict : ——— **FICTION** ———

# There is life on other planets

Are there aliens out there? Well, before we ask that question we've got to work out what we mean by alien life. Scientists would say that it means anything from little green men whizzing around in flying saucers to tiny bacteria, too small to see, clinging to a lump of asteroid. With such a big range of life to look for, is it really believable that we are all alone in this universe of ours? Surely at least one of those billions of stars must have a planet orbiting it with some kind of life on it.

## And the truth is...

We've not found anything yet, but scientists are still looking. A couple of years ago it looked as if life had been found. A meteorite that had landed on Earth had what looked like remains of ancient space bacteria — but that seems to have been a false alarm.

Instead scientists have been concentrating their search on planets roughly similar to Earth, orbiting at a similar kind of distance from a star as Earth does from the Sun. The reason for this is that many scientists believe that Earth has the perfect conditions for life as we know it. Earth has water and isn't too hot or too cold, which gives rise to the nickname for planets like Earth — 'Goldilocks planets'.

For many years the difficulty was finding planets like ours. Many planets are made of gas, like Jupiter, so don't have a proper surface. Others are in the wrong place. However, scientists now know of at least 54 planets similar to Earth.

Another interesting discovery was found here on Earth. A new form of bacteria was found that could live in conditions that we didn't think anything could live in before. This means there could be alien life out there in places where we haven't been looking. Watch this erm...space!

Verdict : — **FICTION** — for now

157

## Eating fish makes you brainy

*'Eat up your fish, it'll make you brainy.'*

This is a popular saying among grandmothers who are determined to make you eat boiled mackerel, pickled herring, battered dogfish or some other delicious fishy dinner.

## ★ And the truth is...

Granny knows best. Oily fish such as mackerel, tuna, salmon, sardines and herring all contains lots of fatty acids. Research in the USA, UK and elsewhere has shown that these can improve your concentration and memory. Just three months of increased consumption of fatty acids leads to improvements in school results. So, if you have exams coming up in three months or longer, get down to the fishmonger's and place your order!

Verdict :

The formula for coke is a closely guarded secret and no one knows the whole recipe

Coca-Cola is one of the most popular and successful fizzy drinks in the world and of course the company doesn't want other soft drinks manufacturers to discover how to make the same drink.

One story says that the secret is so carefully guarded that only two people at Coke are allowed to know the formula. Not only that, but each of them only knows part of the formula. So in fact, no one has the entire recipe for how to make Coke.

## ⭐ And the truth is...

This doesn't really make sense. What would happen if, for example, one of the two Coke employees were killed in a plane crash? His or her part of the formula would be lost. How does it work when one of the employees leaves the company, or retires? If they then tell the formula to someone else, that makes at least three or four people who know it.

Verdict :  **FICTION**

# I'd never have guessed...

## ... that ferrets can get depressed

**Many of us think of ferrets as the smelly, violent thugs of the rodent world. It's not true — ferrets are actually very entertaining, and people have been keeping them as pets for at least 2,000 years.**

Ferrets are extremely playful. When excited they 'dance' sideways, twisting and jumping, while making soft hissing sounds or 'chuckling'. Some ferrets even turn somersaults. But they also have a sensitive side. If they're separated from a companion, ferrets can fall into a depression. They don't want to play, they stop eating and just lie around and sleep all day!

## Lobsters scream when you cook them

**ARGHH!**

Any chef will tell you that a lobster has to be eaten fresh. If you kill it and leave it lying around for a while, it will go off. That's why seafood restaurants often have live lobsters wandering around in a tank, waiting to be cooked. (It's the kind of waiting room you never want to find yourself in...)

The trouble with cooking a live lobster is that when you put it in boiling water, it makes a terrible high-pitched noise. And it's hard to enjoy a plate of lobster when ten minutes before, you heard it screaming with pain as it was boiled to death.

### ★ But the truth is...

No one knows for sure whether lobsters feel pain, but one thing *is* for sure: they can't scream. Lobsters don't have vocal cords or lungs like humans do, so it would be impossible for them. The noise they make when being cooked is just hot air escaping from their shells.

Verdict :  **FICTION**

# CELEBRITY
# GOSSIP
## from long ago

## Rumour has it that Vlad the Impaler was Dracula the vampire!

Vlad III ruled southern Romania in the 15th century and was probably one of the cruellest people ever. He is thought to have killed as many as 100,000 people. But it's the way he finished people off that is particularly gruesome. Each victim was sat (or impaled) on a long spike and then left there. Gravity pulled them down, while the spike worked its way upwards until at last it popped out just under their chin. It was a long, slow death.

Vlad sometimes impaled a few people at the same time. Just for fun.

After his death, Vlad III became known as Vlad the Impaler. But he did have another name. He was also known as Vlad Dracula — but you can put away the wooden stake and the bunch of garlic. Although Vlad was a nasty piece of work, he was not a vampire. His father Vlad II was known as Vlad Dracul, which means 'Vlad the devil'. So Dracula simply means 'son of the devil'.

However, Vlad *did* have a nasty habit of dunking bread in the blood of his victims and then eating it, which is perhaps what gave Victorian author Bram Stoker the idea for his 1897 novel, *Dracula*.

# Swimmers shave their legs to go faster

Athletes who compete in many different types of sport shave their legs — both the women and the men. Most people think this is because the hair slows the athletes down. This seems logical enough — after all, have you ever seen a hairy racing car? Or think about the fastest animals — cheetahs, race horses, greyhounds. They don't exactly have big shaggy coats do they?

## ★ And the truth is...

Athletes shave for different reasons. Bodybuilders do it to look good. Cyclists do it in case they fall off their bikes — it makes patching their legs up easier. Swimmers do it because it makes a tiny difference to their speed as they travel through the water. Is it worth it? Well the difference between first and second in a swimming race is sometimes as little as one hundredth of a second, so the quick answer is yes!

Verdict : ————————

## Meteorites are boiling hot when they hit the ground

Have you ever seen a shooting star streaking across the night sky? In reality what you were seeing was probably a meteor — a piece of space rock burning up as it travels through the Earth's atmosphere. The heat is generated by the speed the meteor is travelling and the friction that is caused by the air. So, all that heat must make the rock hot, right?

## ⭐ And the truth is...

Space is really cold, so space rocks are really cold too. A quick blast through the Earth's atmosphere isn't enough to warm them right through. Also, the outside layer gets blasted off as it burns so by the time the meteor hits the ground — and becomes a meteorite, the name scientists call meteors on the ground — it should be cool.

Verdict :

'This "telephone" has too many shortcomings to be seriously considered as a means of communication. The device is of no value to us.'

Stated in a report in 1876 by Western Union, the telegraph company, on whether they should try and get into the telephone business.

By 1877 Western Union had changed their minds and decided to set up the American Speaking Telephone company. This would become part of the American Bell company, which by 1900 would have almost a million phones in service!

# Mobile phones can blow up petrol stations

Ever since mobile phones first appeared, stories have said that you mustn't use them in a petrol station. The act of turning a phone on, or taking a call, can cause the phone's battery to spark. This spark could set light to the petrol fumes, causing a massive action-movie-style inferno.

 ## And the truth is...

Mobile phones do use batteries, that bit's true. But then again, so do cars — and it's obviously safe to turn on your car in a petrol station, or the whole filling-up-with-petrol system would break down. And in fact, when have you ever seen a spark coming out of a mobile phone?

Because people have claimed there's a theoretical possibility of mobiles triggering a fire, many filling stations have signs forbidding mobile use. But we haven't found any confirmed examples of a mobile actually causing a fire.

Whatever the truth is, though, this urban myth is so widespread that it's a good idea to put your phone away whenever you're near a filling station. Otherwise people might start staring at you, tutting, telling you not to be so irresponsible!

Verdict : almost certainly  but put your phone away anyway

# Cockroaches would survive a nuclear war

The idea behind this myth is that cockroaches would be the only living things to survive a nuclear war. Almost everyone has heard this said, and hardly anyone knows whether it's true or not.

## ★ The truth is...

Cockroaches are very tough: if there were to be a nuclear war, they'd survive a lot longer than humans. But the last creatures left alive would almost certainly be bacteria, which are very adaptable and can live almost anywhere.

Verdict : **FICTION**

## ⭐ 5 things you (probably) didn't know about OCTOPUSES

**1** Octopuses have three hearts.

**2** An octopus weighing about the same as a 10-year-old can squeeze through a hole the size of a tennis ball.

**3** An octopus's eyes have rectangular pupils (the black bits).

**4** If a predator pulls off an octopus's arm, it can escape and re-grow another one later.

**5** Octopuses can use their tentacles to open jam jars, or to hold stones like hammers for opening shellfish!

## Cleopatra died by asp-bite

Cleopatra famously finished herself off by holding an asp to her skin. When the creature took a bite, she is said to have died from the poisonous venom that flowed into her bloodstream.

### ★ And the truth is...

According to the great William Shakespeare, this is what Cleopatra is supposed to have said to the deadly asp.

*'With thy sharp teeth this knot intrinsicate*
*Of life at once untie: poor venomous fool*
*Be angry, and dispatch.'*

But as Shakespeare was basing his story on that of an ancient Greek biographer called Plutarch, it's probably best to rewind time further to find out what he said. And Plutarch did say that Cleopatra suffered death-by-asp. Except... Plutarch lived 130 years after Cleopatra died. So how would he know what happened? In fact, there's a whole range of explanations as to how and why Cleopatra died and not all of them to do with venomous snakes.

In 2010, a German historian called Christoph Schaefer announced that he had read a lot of ancient texts and spoken to a lot of toxicologists — experts in poison — and finally he had the answer. Cleopatra had actually died from a mixture of deadly poisons. And not an asp.

Verdict : _____ Probably **FICTION** — though we may never know for sure

## So what's an asp anyway?

An asp is simply a venomous snake found in the region of the River Nile. Experts think that the one that was supposed to have chomped on Cleopatra would have been the magnificent Egyptian cobra.

# You taste food with your nose

Your nose is really useful; it's particularly good at smelling stuff and as the place you can go snot mining for bogies. Your tongue is very useful too; in particular for tasting things and for sticking out at people you don't like. So there we have it: nose for smelling, tongue for tasting.

## ⭐ And the truth is...

Although you taste with your tongue, the tongue does a fairly basic job. It can tell the difference between sweet, sour, bitter, salty and umami (a kind of savoury taste) — and that's it. It's actually the nose's job to flesh out the tastes, by giving you the smell. Your nose can recognise thousands of different smells, and the brain uses this information along with the taste information to give you the full picture of what you're eating.

If you don't believe this then eat something when you have a blocked nose — your food won't taste half as good.

Verdict : ————  ————

## You lose most of your body heat through your head

On a cold day the best advice is to wear a hat as you lose up to 45% of your body heat through your head. It's such good advice that the US army researched it and put it into one of their training manuals in 1970.

### ⭐ And the truth is...

The results of an experiment are only as good as the experiment itself. The army experiment involved dressing soldiers in Arctic gear and then making them really cold. The results showed that most heat was lost through the head — but that's because it was the only uncovered part of their bodies. If the soldiers had simply worn big furry hats and underpants, most body heat would have been lost from their torso, arms and legs.

Your head doesn't lose heat any faster than anywhere else — but it's still a good idea to wear a hat when it's cold.

## Verdict : —— **FICTION** ——

# Don't use the toilet when the train is in the station!

This urban myth is very well known. In fact, if you ever see anyone emerging from a train toilet at the station, they will almost certainly look embarrassed at having been caught using it. But why?

The answer is that when you flush a train toilet, all the waste is just dumped onto the track. People waiting at the platform will then find themselves sniffing the smell of wee — or worse.

## ★ And the truth is...

How true this is depends on the type of train carriage. Old-fashioned trains will just have a hatch in the floor, which opens when the toilet is flushed. Some designs mix the waste with sterilizing fluids. The most modern trains hold toilet waste on board until they reach the end of the line, when it is pumped out.

Verdict : ___Letter safe than sorry___

## Yawning is infectious

Have you ever noticed that as soon as one person in a group yawns, others start to do the same thing? People will tell you that it's because yawning is infectious. But why would you 'catch' a yawn from someone, when you're not even tired?

 ## The truth is...

Many scientific studies have shown that yawning is indeed infectious. It's also something people do without thinking. They see someone else yawning, and their body just joins in. Scientists have only recently begun to understand why. The answer lies in our prehistoric past.

Yawning gets extra oxygen into the bloodstream. The oxygen helps the muscles and brain get energy, making us better able to move and think quickly. That's why you yawn when tired, to perk yourself up. Our ancient ancestors would have needed a boost like this when under threat — if a dangerous animal was around, for example. If one person yawned to get ready for action, the other members of the band would subconsciously know that they needed to be ready too, and would yawn — and that's why we do the same.

Verdict : 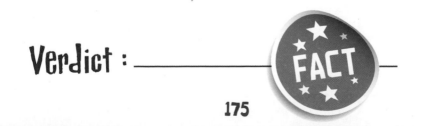 FACT

# When animals ATTACK!

## Escaping a big cat

No, we don't mean that large Siamese from down the road — we mean cats like leopards, tigers and lions. They generally like to creep up on their prey from behind, but if you do spot one stalking you, how do you avoid becoming lunch?

 Don't run away — this tells the cat you're prey, and it will attack.

Stare at it — in the cat world, this is a sign of aggression. Who knows, maybe it will back down?

Make yourself look as big as possible, and shout as loudly as you can without sounding panicky.

If an attack happens, fight back with a stick or rocks.

A lizard grows a new tail if the old one gets left behind

OK, by 'left behind', we actually mean ripped off by a predator. There's a long-standing belief that if a lizard's tail is grabbed by an attacker, and it has a choice between:

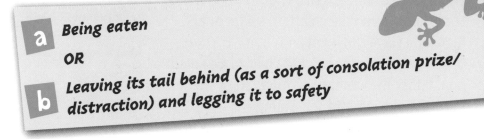

**a** Being eaten

OR

**b** Leaving its tail behind (as a sort of consolation prize/ distraction) and legging it to safety

the lizard will choose option 'b' every time.

Not only that — in a short space of time the lizard will have grown a brand-new tail, ready for the next great escape.

## And the truth is...

One of the most common types of lizard is known as a skink. They're small creatures about 10 cm long. Usually about half a skink's length is made up of its long, pointy tail. Most skink tails are designed to snap off if pulled on hard, then wriggle about on their own for a few seconds. New tails do grow but don't grow back completely, though.

Verdict : ———— basically  FACT

# Viking chiefs were cremated on their longships

It wasn't just the Viking chief's body that was burned — the longship was piled with stuff that he might need in the next life. This included food, beer, clothes, weapons, jewellery, dogs and horses. Sometimes, even the chieftain's wife or his favourite slave girl went with him. Unfortunately for them, they had to be killed first. Either the woman volunteered or she was dragged to the ship, kicking and screaming.

## ★ And the truth is...

It sounds a bit extreme, doesn't it? But it's all true. The Vikings believed that a ship would carry the dead safely on their journey to the next life and they gave their chiefs a magnificent send-off.

Viking funerals took place by rivers or near the coast. And then, once the longship was loaded up with bodies and belongings, it was set adrift on the water. A relative of the chief threw the first firebrand and then the other mourners joined in. Blazing brightly, the longship would sail away.

Verdict : —————————

## The walls of medieval houses were made of cow poo

Ick. Urgh. Gross. Not even the three little pigs made their houses out of cow poo. Surely this is far too disgusting to be true? But take a closer look at some of those pretty Elizabethan houses from the very olden days and you might be surprised.

 **And the truth is...**

The walls *were* made of cow poo, at least partly anyway. There were quite a lot of other ingredients too. Technically, the construction technique is called wattle and daub — it was first used in the Stone Age and has been found in Europe, Asia, Africa and the Americas. Wooden strips are woven together to make a lattice called wattle and this is daubed with a sticky mixture of soil, clay, sand, straw and — hold your nose — animal dung. All gaps in the wattle must be filled to make sure that the wall is solid. Once it's dry, the wattle and daub is often whitewashed to make it more waterproof.

Verdict :  _____

179

# Light travels at

How fast is fast? Running is faster than walking, for example, but racing cars are faster than running. Take the quiz below to see if you can work out who is faster.

**Rank these in order of fastest to slowest:**

Cheetah

Three-toed sloth

Olympic sprinter

Peregrine falcon

Snail

Racehorse

**Answers:**

Peregrine falcon 320 km/hr (200 mph)

Cheetah 100 km/hr (65 mph)

Racehorse 60 km/hr (37 mph)

Olympic sprinter 37 km/h (23 mph)

Snail 0.42 km/h (0.26 mph)

Sloth 0.24 km/h (0.15 mph)

# 300,000 km/hr

So, although an Olympic sprinter might seem unbelievably quick to a sloth, the peregrine falcon puts them all in the shade. But what about light? It might seem odd to talk about the speed of light at all. You switch on a light switch, and the light is there immediately. Or is it?

Actually the light seems to be there straight away because light is travelling from the light bulb to your eyes unbelievably quickly — speeds that a falcon could only dream of travelling. But how fast is fast — 300,000 km/hr?

 **And the truth is...**

Light travels much, much quicker than that — around 300,000 km per second. It is quite probable that nothing travels faster than light.

Although this means that light reaches you almost immediately from a light bulb, this is not true when you look at the huge distances between objects in space. For example, the Sun is around 150 million km (92 million miles) away from Earth. This means that the Sun's light takes roughly 8 minutes to reach the Earth. The light from distant stars can take months to get to Earth — imagine how long a sloth would take!

Verdict :_____

# Health-related inventions you've probably never heard of before

Over the years there have been lots of crazy health-related inventions that seemed — mistakenly — like a good idea at the time. Here are our top picks:

## 1 Eyeball massager

Looking like a crazy pair of binoculars, this device puffed cool air on to your eyeballs, which presumably was a relaxing treatment for tired eyes.

## 2 Finger stretcher

Aimed at pianists who hoped to give their fingers a wider range on the keyboard, this was presumably also bought by amateur torturers.

## 3 Spectacles with lights

See in the dark with these amazing spectacles that have tiny lights on top! Just don't go out in the rain, unless you want an electric shock.

# You should never wake a sleepwalker

Lots of people will tell you that you should never wake a sleepwalker. You'll hear various reasons for this:

 **The sleepwalker will have a heart attack**
The shock of being woken up in a strange place will be so great that the sleeping person's heart will stop.

 **They will have a seizure or fit**
The brain, suddenly wrenched from sleep, will go haywire, causing the sleepwalker to have a fit.

**3 They will attack you**
Surprised and confused, woken sleepwalkers can sometimes lash out and attack the person who has woken them up.

## ★ And the truth is...
It's actually quite difficult to wake a sleepwalker, but there's no health reason not to do it. The person may be surprised and disoriented, though, so it's best to try and gently lead them back to bed without waking them.

Verdict :

## You can get rid of leeches by burning them off

Like sucking the venom out of a snakebite (see pages 56-57), this was once a standard feature in movies. Almost any jungle scene would feature people having to wade through waist-deep water, then finding their legs were covered in leeches. The next steps were:

1. Light a match.
2. Touch it to the leech.
3. Listen to the sizzle.
4. Watch leech drop off.

Would this be a good idea in real life?

## ⭐ The truth is...

No, it wouldn't. Firstly, what are you doing with matches, you dummy? You may well burn yourself and everyone knows it's really dangerous to play with fire. Second, the leech WILL let go — but it will also vomit into the cut it's made in your skin. This is likely to cause an infection.

The best way to get rid of a leech is to slide your fingernail under each of its three suckers, making it fall off.

Verdict : **FICTION**

# DOgs can smell fear

You most often hear this from someone who's not at all afraid of dogs. Usually they're saying it to someone who is afraid of dogs. But is it true, can dogs really smell fear?

## ⭐ The truth is...

Dogs have incredibly sensitive noses. They can smell the difference between every single human they've ever met (apart from identical twins). They can smell cancer cells with more accuracy than million-dollar scanning machines. They can even smell tiny changes in the air when electricity is present. So it's really not surprising that dogs can also smell chemicals in your sweat, which are released when you're nervous or fearful!

Verdict : _____

## The Curse of the Pharaohs means certain death for tomb visitors!

In 1922, archaeologist and Egyptologist Howard Carter and his team discovered the tomb of Tutankhamun in the Valley of the Kings. Their eyes goggled because the tomb was overflowing with ancient treasures. But bad luck followed. Lord Carnarvon, who was funding the excavation, was bitten by a mosquito and died when the wound became infected. One of the team died from fever, one was shot by his wife, one died from blood poisoning and one death was totally unexplained… Within a year, five of those who had witnessed the opening of the tomb were dead. People seriously began to believe that the deaths were all caused by the Curse of the Pharaohs. They had disturbed a mummy's tomb — and they were paying with their lives.

## ⭐ And the truth is...

There has never been any actual evidence of a curse inside a pharaoh's tomb. It was all just rumour that was hyped further by the media when Lord Carnarvon died.

But why did so many people die so quickly? It might have been something to do with deadly bacteria contained within the tomb. But it was probably pure coincidence. Perhaps the most compelling evidence that there was never any curse is Howard Carter himself. It is true that he died after the tomb was opened, but it was 17 years later, when he was 64.

Verdict :  **FICTION**

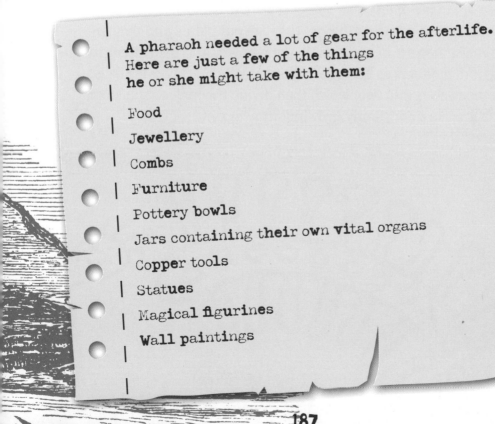

A pharaoh needed a lot of gear for the afterlife. Here are just a few of the things he or she might take with them:

Food

Jewellery

Combs

Furniture

Pottery bowls

Jars containing their own vital organs

Copper tools

Statues

Magical figurines

Wall paintings

# Bacteria are good for you

'Have you washed your hands?'

'It's covered in germs!'

'Don't eat that, it's dirty!'

Ever heard this? It's pretty good advice, after all bacteria can be truly deadly. It's amazing to think that something so small — bacteria are made of just one, single cell — can be so harmful. But then, bacteria are amazing things. They are not plants and they are not animals, they are in a group all of their own. And their strength comes from numbers as bacteria multiply really quickly — the cells divide themselves into two, which then divide themselves and so on. Bacteria are like a constantly growing army of evil.

## ⭐ And the truth is...

There are plenty of different types of bacteria out there which can do you harm. Doctors call them pathogens. But without bacteria we'd be in a lot of trouble, too. Our intestines are full of them and without them we wouldn't be able to digest a lot of the things we eat. Good bacteria also help our immune systems to stay healthy. And some of the bacteria in our food make it taste the way it does. You couldn't make cheese and yogurt, for example, without bacteria.

So, some bacteria are bad, some are good and some are just downright tasty.

Verdict : _____

FACT

## It's possible for a man to become pregnant

Just a few years ago, the world was amazed to hear that a person named Lee Mingwei had become the first man to get pregnant.

The story said that after having hormone treatment, Mr Lee had a human embryo implanted in his belly. There, it would grow into a baby before being removed by Caesarian section.

Incredibly, a website gave details, including photos of the pregnant Mr Lee. You could even see ultrasound images of the baby inside him. So it must be true, right?

## ★ And the truth is...

The misguided genius behind the project was an artist named Virgil Wong. He and his friend Lee Mingwei put the whole story together themselves. They claimed that it was art — maybe the question here should really be, are they right?

Verdict : _____  **FICTION** _____

190

# The Coca-Cola company invented the modern Santa Claus

Everybody loves Santa Claus. When that jolly, plump man with the white beard and the red-and-white outfit starts appearing on billboards and in TV ads, we know Christmas is on its way.

There's a well-known urban myth that says most people don't realise there's a secret message hidden in the images of the modern Santa, and that message is: 'Buy more Coke.' How can this be so? Well, it's because the modern Santa Claus — the white-bearded man in a red outfit — was created by Coca-Cola. You can tell because they painted him in their own colours, red and white, as an advertising logo!

## ⭐ And the truth is...

Coke did not invent the modern Santa. In fact, he first appeared in a Coke ad in 1930, and red-and-white Santas had been around for at least 30 years by then.

Verdict : ___  ___

# ☆ 5 things you (probably) didn't know about LIONS

**1** Lions often sleep for up to 20 hours a day!

**2** They cannot roar until they're two years old – but once they can, it can be heard up to 8 km away.

**3** Male lions are very lazy: females do 90% of the hunting.

**4** No two male lions have the same pattern of whiskers on their muzzles.

**5** Lions are lucky to live beyond 10 years in the wild.

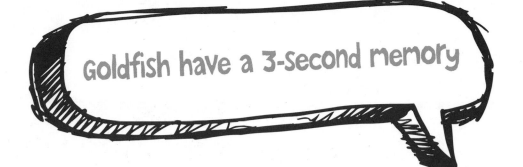

# Goldfish have a 3-second memory

Everyone — especially if they own a goldfish — loves this fact. It makes goldfish owners feel better about keeping their pet in a teeny-tiny tank that it takes only a matter of seconds to swim around.

The idea is that the goldfish never gets bored, because by the time he's swum around his bowl the goldfish has forgotten that he's already seen the plastic castle 2,925 times in the last three hours and 15 minutes.

Do I know you from somewhere?

## ⭐ But the truth is...

Goldfish actually have quite good memories (compared to other fish, anyway). They have been taught to push levers, fetch things and do various other tricks. They seem to be able to remember skills they've learned for anything up to a year.

Verdict :  **FICTION**

# EWW, IT CAN'T BE TRUE!

## Mummies were embalmed in open-air tents because the whiff was so bad.

If you've ever been on holiday to Egypt, or you know someone who has, you'll also know that it's VERY hot. The same was true in Ancient Egyptian times, which made it rather tricky to prepare a Pharaoh for the afterlife without the dead body ponging a bit. OK, a lot. To make it more pleasant for the embalmer, who had the unenviable job of cutting out the Pharaoh's vital organs and then yanking out the brain through the nose with a hook, they popped him in an open-air tent. Here, the fresh air meant that the body might not smell quite so bad for the 40 days it took to dry out.

### Did you know...?

Some Egyptian mummies had onions for eyes! Embalmers took out the eyeballs and replaced them with onions. History doesn't tell us whether they were pickled or not, though these would have stayed fresh longer.

## Thomas Edison invented the light bulb

The light bulb was one of the most hotly contested innovations of the 19th century. At one point, it seemed like nearly *everyone* had invented it. And Thomas Edison shouted loudest of all. So was it *really* him who did it?

Before the winner is announced, take a look at the three main contenders for the title of **Inventor of the Light Bulb**.

First up, we have **Humphry Davy**! This brilliant British chemist invented the Davy lamp — an electric lamp that allowed miners to illuminate underground workings without danger of igniting the very flammable methane gas that often caused explosions. It worked by creating a spark between two charcoal rods. He was awarded a medal for his invention in 1816 — hurray! — but it was far too bright and used a lot of power — boo! — which meant that it wasn't much use for everyday use. But Davy deserves bonus points for highlighting the very risky conditions in mines. Bravo!

read on!

Next, step forward *Joseph Swan*! The fabulous British physicist spent years working on his light bulbs, sometimes publishing his findings. And at last, in 1878, he showed off his new light bulb. Its carbon filament — fine thread — glowed brightly, but not for long. So he set about making the light bulb better. But did he finish it in time to win the prize…?

And finally, please give it up for *Thomas Edison*! In 1879, this amazingly entrepreneurial American inventor — who probably had access to Swan's earlier findings — patented his own light bulb. By the following year he had improved this light bulb so much that it glowed for a totally brilliant — *geddit?* — 1,200 hours.

Mr Humphry Davy

…and his lamp

## ⭐ And the winner is...

Humphry Davy didn't invent the light bulb, but it was his lamp that really got things started. And Thomas Edison didn't invent the light bulb either — Joseph Swan was officially the Inventor of the Lightbulb — but he did make it much better. Edison was a businessman as well as an inventor and when he saw an opportunity for improving something and making money from it, he went for it. In the end, it didn't really matter that he didn't win the light-bulb race. He became very rich anyway.

Verdict : **FICTION**

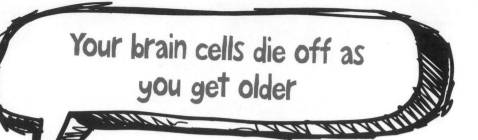

# Your brain cells die off as you get older

Age does terrible things to the human body. Hair falls out from where you want it (your head, mainly) and grows where you don't want it (your nose and ears). Your skin gets wrinkly, your eyesight gets worse, your hearing gets worse, your reaction speeds slow down, and your joints ache. Worse still, from the age of 25 your brain cells start dying off. By the age of 80 it's amazing you can do anything or remember anything at all. Which might be why grown ups are always forgetting stuff!

## ★ And the truth is...

Scientists have discovered that although brain cells die off, people can also regenerate, or grow, new brain cells. The good news doesn't stop there. Once a person gets past middle age, the speed at which one brain cell works with another brain cell actually speeds up. So while the body slows down, the brain works quicker!

Verdict :

## The Sun is the biggest star

We rely on the Sun for light and heat and, by extension, life itself. It's our closest star, lying a mere 150 million km (93 million miles) away, which in space terms is a tiny distance. For example our next nearest star is Proxima Centauri which is around 399 trillion km (248 trillion miles) away. As the Sun is so close it looks much bigger than other stars, which look like small dots of light in the sky.

### ⭐ And the truth is...

Although all those stars look the same to the naked eye there are actually lots of different sizes. There are tiny dwarf stars, medium sized stars, giants and massive supergiants. The Sun is a run-of-the-mill, medium sized star — quite boring in star terms really. But it's our star and we love it.

Verdict :  FICTION

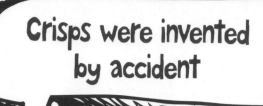

## Crisps were invented by accident

Crisps are one of the world's favourite snacks. Something so delicious must surely have been the result of chefs spending long hours trying to make tasty snacks from potatoes?

Not if the rumours are true. A popular urban myth says that crisps were actually invented by accident, in 1853, by an angry chef named George Crum. A customer had sent back his chips, complaining they were too thick and soggy. The chef decided to get his own back by slicing some potatoes as thin as possible and frying them. To his surprise the picky customer was delighted — and the popularity of the potato crisp had begun.

## ★ The truth is...

Crum was not the first person to make crisps. There were similar recipes in several cookbooks years before his 1853 'discovery'.

Verdict : _____  FICTION _____

## An office worker died at his desk and no one noticed for days

George Turklebaum, this urban myth says, was a worker at a New York publishing company. George kept to himself, but was a dedicated worker. He was usually first to the office in the morning, and last to leave at night. He would often spend hours hunched over his desk, checking through papers.

Perhaps it's not surprising that George's fellow workers didn't immediately notice that he hadn't moved much at his desk one day. What is surprising, though, is that it took them five days to notice that he was still in the exact-same position. George wasn't just concentrating really hard. He was dead.

⭐ **And the truth is...**

Except in very cold conditions, bodies start to decompose in a lot less than five days. In fact, within three days George would have started to whiff and unpleasant fluids would have started to leak from his body.

On top of that, at the time this story appeared, there was no George Turklebaum listed in the New York phone book.

Verdict : _____ **FICTION** ___

## Chameleons change colour for camouflage

Everyone knows that chameleons can change colour. People will tell you it's a defence technique, which allows the lizards to blend in with their background. They can match rocks, leaves, sand and all sorts of other natural environments. But is this well-known fact actually true?

### ⭐ The fact is...

First of all, not all chameleons can change colour. Some are very happy staying the same colour all the time, thank you.

Secondly, the chameleons that can change colour don't really do it for disguise. Sometimes they change to a darker colour when they're cold, as this allows them to absorb more heat. But usually they change colour according to their mood, because they're angry, scared, trying to attract a female, etc.

Verdict :  FICTION

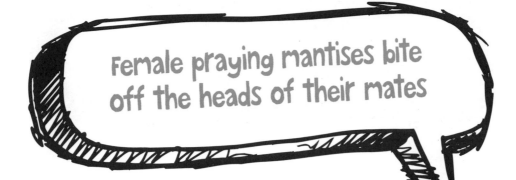

Female praying mantises bite off the heads of their mates

Presumably, if this myth is true, there aren't many second dates in the praying mantis world. For years a rumour has been going around that the female praying mantis bites off the male's head during mating.

Various reasons have been given for this unromantic approach to female/male relations:

- It provides the female with protein, which she needs for the reproductive process.
- Biting the male's head off stops him from leaving before the job is done.
- Having his head bitten off is a signal to the male to release his sperm.

## ★ The truth is...

Mating is a risky business for the male praying mantis, because the female does sometimes bite off his head — but only if she's hungry. It doesn't always happen, and certainly isn't for any of the reasons suggested above.

Verdict :  — but doesn't always happen

## Flesh-eating plants can feed on mammals

Plants — we eat them, feed them to animals or dig them up because we think they're weeds. Not surprising then that the idea of plants getting their revenge and gobbling us up has been a much-used idea in books and films. Although the chances of getting chased down the street by a ferocious dandelion is non-existent; not everything is safe.

### And the truth is...

Carnivorous plants do exist, take the insect eating Venus Flytrap or the sundew for example. Pitcher plants are like living jugs, partly filled with a watery liquid. Animals are attracted to the liquid, then fall in and slowly dissolve — and this is where the plant finds the nutrients which it needs to grow. The larger varieties, such as *Nepenthes attenboroughii* from the Philippines, are big enough to trap snakes, birds and even small mammals such as rats. Yummy.

Verdict :

# Sunlight makes you sneeze

From way back in history, people noticed that moving from the shade into sunlight could make you sneeze. Even the famous Ancient Greek scientist Aristotle wrote about it. Does this mean people can be allergic to the Sun?

## ★ And the truth is...

About one third of the population suffer from what scientists call the photic sneeze reflex. Curiously, no one can say exactly why it happens as no proper studies have been done. Scientists guess that it might have something to do with messages from the eyes getting misinterpreted by the brain. The eyes close slightly in reaction to the sunlight, the brain thinks the nose is irritated, so the person sneezes.

Whatever the reason, wearing sunglasses solves the problem.

Verdict :  FACT

# THE MOON LANDINGS WERE FAKED

Oh boy. There are so many urban myths, legends and conspiracy theories about the Moon Landings that you could fill an entire book with them. In fact, some people have done, in an attempt to show that the landings themselves never took place.

For those of you with more interesting things to spend your time on than an entire book of Moon Landing myths, here's our summary of the main ones:

## 1. The American flag

The American flag is seen waving in the breeze — but there's no wind on the Moon, which does not have an atmosphere.

In fact, the flag only waves about as an astronaut is screwing it into the Moon's surface. The rest of the time it's still.

## 2. No stars

Even though the sky is dark, you cannot see any stars in photos of the Moon Landings.

This is because all landings took place during lunar daytime, with the surface lit up by the Sun's rays (which is why it was possible to take photos in the first place). Stars shine too dimly during lunar daytime to be picked up on film.

## 3. Invisible photographers

When astronaut Neil Armstrong first stepped onto the Moon, he was filmed. But his fellow astronaut Buzz Aldrin was inside the lunar lander. So who was doing the filming?

The footage of Armstrong stepping down on to the surface was shot by an automatic device. It had already been manoeuvred into position.

In some photos of astronaut Buzz Aldrin, you can see from the reflection in his visor that Neil Armstrong isn't holding a camera. So who took that photo?

The astronauts had cameras mounted on their chests, so that they didn't have to hold them in their hands.

## 4. Rockets without flames

When the lunar module took off, no flames appeared to come from its exhaust.

This is because the fuel that was used produces a flame that is transparent, hard to see, and almost impossible to photograph.

Verdict : **FICTION** on all counts

## Elephants are scared of nice

It's a nice idea: one of the world's biggest animals being scared of one of the world's smallest. And it's a idea that is explored in many children's cartoons and movies, too.

But can it be true?

*No, I'm NOT getting out of your way.*

### ⭐ The answer is...

Elephants don't really meet mice in the wild, although they do come across them in captivity. But elephants don't have very good eyesight, so they would be unlikely to even *notice* a mouse — let alone hurry away from it.

Verdict :  **FICTION**

## Camels store water in their humps

Camels are brilliantly adapted for life in the desert.
They have extra-wide feet, which helps them walk across loose sand without sinking in. Their thick coats reflect sunlight and keep out heat, but keep the camels warm at night. Their mouths are able to chew thorny desert plants. And — best of all — they can store water in their humps. Can't they?

## ⭐ The truth is...

Camels *are* brilliantly adapted for desert life*, and their humps are one of these adaptations — but they don't contain water. In fact, the hump contains fat. The camel stores fat in its hump (instead of all over the body like humans do) so that there's no layer of fat to trap heat in the high temperatures of the desert.

*For example, camels release so little moisture through their bodies that camel wee is thick like syrup, and their poo is so dry you can set light to it!

Verdict : **FICTION**

## 'Houston, we have a problem.'

In 1970, the Apollo 13 space mission went spectacularly wrong. An oxygen tank exploded, temperatures plummeted and there was very little power on board the spacecraft. Many believe that when the commander of the spaceflight, Jim Lovell, spoke to mission control in back on Earth, he said, 'Houston, we have a problem.'

The truth is that he actually said, 'Houston, we've had a problem.' (Space fans might like to know that Commander Lovell then said, 'We've had a main B bus undervolt.' This had nothing to do with public transport.) But somehow, no one remembers this. And even if they do, perhaps they actually think that 'Houston, we have a problem' sounds better. Whatever Apollo 13's problem was, it meant that the moon landing was cancelled. But the good news is

that all three astronauts found a way around the problem and made it back to earth safely, splashing down in the Pacific Ocean. And everyone in Houston (and the rest of the world) was delighted.*

*Some of them were so delighted that they made a film called - can you guess? - Apollo 13 in 1995, starring Tom Hanks as Jim Lovell.

## Human beings have five senses

Your senses are your way of knowing where you are and what you are doing. Your five senses are: sight, smell, hearing, taste and touch. The brain receives the information from your senses in the form of electrical impulses which your nerves send when they detect something. These are all your brain needs to know what's going on and how to react to any given situation.

### ★ And the truth is...

Scientists today believe that you might have anywhere between nine and twenty-one senses. These include the ability to feel pain, pressure, temperature and where your limbs are in relation to your own body. You can try this last one very easily: close your eyes and lift your arm up. You know exactly where your arm is, but you're not looking at it and it's not touching anything or being touched.

It seems we need more than five senses after all.

Verdict : _____  _____

# Objects sink because they are heavier than water

Throw a feather in a river and what does it do? It floats of course. Now try it with a stone. It sinks like … well, a stone. The feather is light so it floats; the stone sinks because it's heavy. Job done, what's next?

##  And the truth is...

But hold on a minute, what are big ships made from? Why metal of course. So how do *they* float?

The answer is air. A ship covers a big area with a little bit of metal with lots of air inside it. The combined weight of metal and air is less than the water it sits on, so the ship stays afloat.

So objects sink because they are heavier than water — but heavier than water objects can be made to float!

Verdict :  **FACT** and **FICTION**

# Where In The World?

OK, for a drink to be called 'champagne' it has to come from the Champagne region of France. But the French like to think that they invented this method of making fizzy wine. Specifically, Dom Perignon is said to have developed sparkling wine in the late 1600s.

Shame, then, that Britain's Royal Society heard exactly how to make fizzy wine thirty years earlier, in a paper by a scientist called Christopher Merrit.

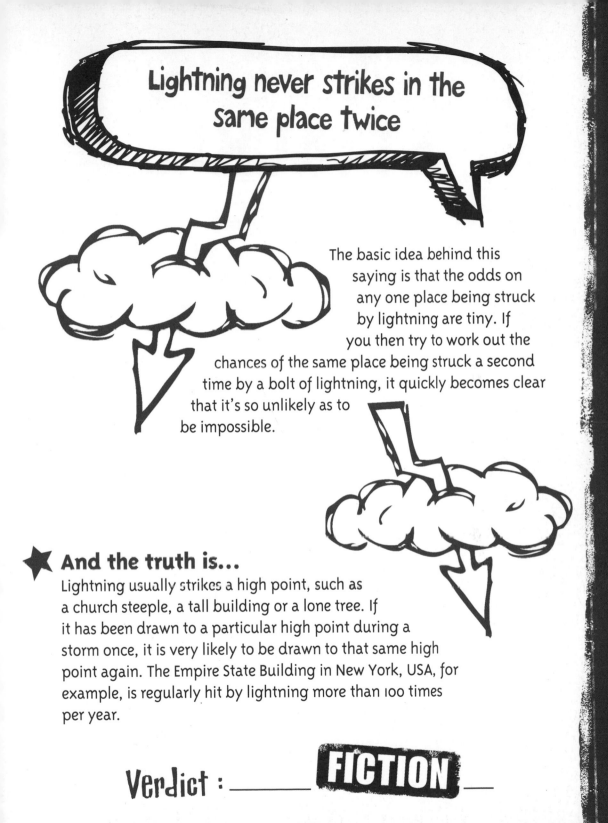

## Lightning never strikes in the same place twice

The basic idea behind this saying is that the odds on any one place being struck by lightning are tiny. If you then try to work out the chances of the same place being struck a second time by a bolt of lightning, it quickly becomes clear that it's so unlikely as to be impossible.

### ★ And the truth is...

Lightning usually strikes a high point, such as a church steeple, a tall building or a lone tree. If it has been drawn to a particular high point during a storm once, it is very likely to be drawn to that same high point again. The Empire State Building in New York, USA, for example, is regularly hit by lightning more than 100 times per year.

Verdict : _____ **FICTION** _

# When animals ATTACK!

## Escaping a bull

Halfway across a field, you suddenly become aware of a very large, angry-looking bull snorting at you.

How do you avoid being torn limb from limb?

 *Stand still! Bulls can't see very well, and if you don't move, it will probably wander off.*

 *If the bull does start to charge, run for it. Bulls can run faster than humans, so aim to get up a tree or behind something before the bull reaches you.*

 *Throw things behind you – maybe a coat you were holding. The bull might stop and investigate it, giving you time to escape.*

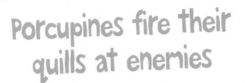

# Porcupines fire their quills at enemies

If you meet a porcupine while out for a walk one day, and it turns its back on you — watch out! It may be preparing to fire its quills at you. At least, that's what plenty of people think.

If true, this would mean porcupines have a brilliant defence system. But does it really exist?

## ⭐ The truth is...

People who believe this myth usually come from places where porcupines don't live. A porcupine's quills are actually thick, stiff hairs. Imagine trying to fire your hair at people. It wouldn't work.

Porcupines do have a great defence system, though. The quills have barbed ends. If an animal tries to bite the porcupine it turns round. The attacker gets a face full of quills, which are not fired but break off. The quills hook into the flesh and often become infected.

Verdict : _____ **FICTION** _____

**217**

## The Greeks hid inside the wooden horse of Troy

In Greek mythology, the Trojan War was a long war between Troy and Sparta. It all began because Paris of Troy fell in love with Helen and whisked her away from her husband Menelaus, the King of Sparta (a city state in Greece). Menelaus wanted his wife back, so he gathered an enormous fleet of ships and sailed to Troy to fetch her. But Paris refused to give Helen up, so Menelaus besieged the city.

After ten years and many deaths, the Greeks came up with the brilliant idea of building a huge wooden horse and using it to get inside the sturdy city walls of Troy.

A few soldiers were chosen to hide inside the wooden creature, while the rest of them sailed a short distance away and hid. Thrilled that the Greeks had gone at last, but curious about the enormous horse, the Trojans pulled it inside their city. That night, the Greeks crept out of their hiding place and sailed back to Troy in darkness. They flung open the gates of Troy and rushed inside. The city of Troy was doomed.

## And the truth is...

No one really knows if the Trojan War ever happened or not. Greek poet Homer wrote about the events in his epic poems the *Iliad* and the *Odyssey*, but this may have been a few hundred years later. Also, the Trojan War is part of Greek mythology. As well as featuring a host of famous names — Paris, Hector, Achilles and Helen, the most beautiful woman in the world — it also starred Greek gods and goddesses too. So the entire war may just have been a story... Except, in 1870, German archaeologist Heinrich Schliemann found the remains of an ancient city that could have been Troy.

So if the city of Troy existed, perhaps the war took place too. Because the Greek city states did have a reputation for war. And if the war took place, perhaps they even had a wooden horse...

Verdict : Probably **FICTION** but maybe, just maybe, this was the TRUTH...

# Galileo invented the telescope

Galileo made a number of famous discoveries with his telescope. He studied the Moon and noted how it was made of high regions and flat 'seas'. He was the first person to see some of the moons around Jupiter. He also studied Venus and even the Sun. Almost as remarkable as his discoveries is the fact that he made his telescope himself.

## ★ And the truth is...

Although Galileo did make his own telescope, he wasn't the first person to do so. It's unclear where the idea originated, but historians think it may have been a German-Dutch man called Hans Lippershey, who made the first ones in 1608.

Galileo made his own versions, but being the clever so-and-so that he was he did it without actually seeing what one of the existing telescopes looked like. He simply heard about what a telescope could do and figured out how it worked. And by all accounts Galileo's telescopes were the best in the world at the time. Galileo had taken that most important second step — he had taken an invention and improved on it.

Verdict :

## You use more muscles frowning than smiling

You have muscles all over your body — which is a good thing as without them you wouldn't move. However, you probably have a heck of a lot more of them than you think. For example, did you know that you have 43 muscles in just your face? This might seem a lot but think about all the many little movements you can make: eyebrows raising, eyelids shutting, nostrils flaring, mouth opening and closing and so on and so on. All these movements rely on more than one muscle, and that's true for smiling as well as frowning.

## ⭐ And the truth is:

You use twelve facial muscles to make a genuine smile and eleven to pull a frown. This might make it sound like it takes less effort to look grumpy, but it seems that the muscles you use to smile are used more often than the frowning muscles so are more used to doing the work. In short, smiling is easier, but uses more muscle.

Verdict : —— **FICTION** —

## Eating carrots helps you to see in the dark

Generations of children know this urban myth well!

No one knows how many carrots have died a horrible death, being slowly boiled in steaming water, so that children won't need glasses. It must be millions. But did those innocent little carrots die needlessly?

## ★ The truth is...

Flight Lieutenant John Cunningham — sometimes called 'Cat's Eyes Cunningham' — knew the answer to this one. He became famous in Britain during the Second World War (1939-45) for his amazing ability to spot German bombers at night. It was said that this was partly due to Cunningham's love of carrots. People were so impressed with the idea that they started eating extra carrots, hoping it would help them find their way around during the night-time blackout.

Unfortunately, the whole thing was made up. The British were actually spotting German bombers using a new kind of radar, which they didn't want the enemy to find out about. The carrot story was just a distraction. pure fabrication!

Verdict : ___ **FICTION** ___

## strawberry milkshakes contain crushed beetles

Next time you order a strawberry milkshake, should you worry that you'll actually be drinking down little particles of crushed-up beetle? That's what this urban myth says — but surely modern food safety laws mean this can't possibly be the case?

### ★ And the truth is...

It's not just strawberry milkshakes! Lots of the red-coloured things you drink or eat may contain crushed beetle.

Hundreds of years ago, people in Central and South America worked out that the ground-up remains of a certain kind of beetle, which lived in a particular type of cactus, could be used to dye things red. The dye is now called cochineal, and it is still used in lots of red food and drinks.

Verdict : _____

FACT

# Giant alligators lurk in New York's sewers

Every once in a while, an *actual* alligator of some sort pops up on the streets of New York City, USA. In just the last few years:

> A small caiman* was caught wandering around among the picnicking families in Central Park. It had been living in one of the lakes.

> Another caiman was captured by the cops outside an apartment building in Brooklyn, after hissing and snapping at them in an effort to resist arrest.

> An alligator was spotted lurking under a parked car in Queens, only to be scooped up by the long arm of the law.

All these reptiles were tiddlers, less than a metre long. But stories suggest that down in the sewers, far bigger monsters may be lurking…

Stories about alligators in New York's sewers have been around for nearly 100 years. In the 1930s a former city official called Teddy May told of having seen colonies of alligators — some of them huge — living in the sewers.

*A smaller, slimmer relative of the alligator, originally from Central or South America.

Where did these alligators come from? The story goes that people who had visited Florida brought them to the city as pets. But the alligators grew, as alligators do. They were either let go at night or, if small enough, flushed down the toilet.

Once down in the sewers the alligators thrived. They grew bigger and bigger, met other alligators, had babies, and generally took over. Pretty soon it was a brave sewer worker who went into the darkest, deepest parts of the system.

Ahhhh, this is the life...

## ⭐ And the truth is...

Oddly, in 1935 a 2.5-metre alligator *was* caught in the sewers. It can't have been living there for long, though — alligators are cold-blooded and need warmth to survive, but New York's sewers are freezing in winter. Also, an alligator would probably find it impossible to survive the pollution down there.

Verdict : **FICTION**

# EWW, IT CAN'T BE TRUE!

## Ancient Greeks and Romans used pig and ox bladders as footballs.

First, they blew the bladder up like a balloon and then they stuffed it with leaves and hair. Unfortunately, these footballs punctured quite easily (so a World Cup squad would have found it very difficult to sign one without bursting it). So now they're made of plastic and rubber, which is way less yucky.

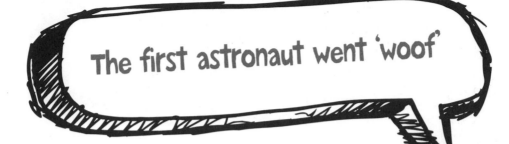

# The first astronaut went 'woof'

(And no, this doesn't mean that they went up in flames.)

Ha ha! How totally ridiculous! It sounds like something that would happen in a pantomime. One of the world's great superpowers sent a dog into space?
*Oh no, they didn't.*

## ⭐ And the truth is...

*Oh yes, they did.*

In the 1950s, Soviet scientists did not know whether it was possible for a human to survive a launch into space. And as they didn't want to test the theory with a real, live person, they decided to send a dog into space instead. A stray named Laika was chosen for this important job and on 3 November 1957, she rocketed into space on board *Sputnik 2*. Laika became the first creature to go to space and the first to orbit Earth, but sadly she died from overheating after a few hours. In Moscow, there stands a statue of a rocket with a dog perched on top to remember her.

Verdict : _____

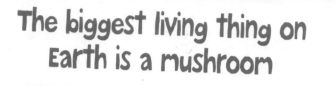

# The biggest living thing on Earth is a mushroom

It's easy to take plants for granted; they're just there — they don't move, they can't speak, or bark or growl. They make rubbish pets. Some have flowers, some don't. Some have leaves, some don't. And that's about as exciting as it gets... Except for the fact that plants do some truly remarkable things. Take bamboo for instance; it grows at incredible speed — up to 38 cm (24 in) in a day — that's almost fast enough to see. Or take *Euphorbia* whose seed pods actually explode in order to shoot their seeds over as wide an area as possible. Or take Venus Flytraps and pitcher plants that actually eat animals (see page 204). Or take the giant redwood trees which can grow up to an amazing 110m (364 ft), which is twice the height of Nelson's column in London. Surely nothing is bigger than that?

## ⭐ And the truth is...

Although at least four species of tree reach over 91m (300 ft), the redwood is indeed the tallest species of plant in the world. But it isn't the biggest. That honour belongs to a variety of the honey mushroom, a fungus called *Armillaria ostoyae* — and it makes a redwood look like a toothpick. A specimen of this fungus was found in Oregon, USA, and it covered an area of 965 hectares (2,384 acres), which is roughly the size of 1,590 football pitches.

You would think something as big as that would be easy to spot, but most of the plant lives underground with occasional clumps of mushrooms sprouting up here and there.

This amazing plant holds another record. It could be up to 8,650 years old, which would make it also the oldest living thing on the planet!

Verdict :

# Elvis is ALIVE!

Elvis Presley was the best-selling music star of all time. He had ten US number one albums, and many more in other countries. His singles topped the charts 18 times in the US and 21 times in the UK. US President Jimmy Carter once said that Elvis had:

*'Changed the face of American... culture.'*

When Elvis died in 1977, roughly 80,000 people lined the streets between his home at Graceland and the Forest Hill Cemetery in Tennessee, USA. They couldn't believe he had died at just 42 years of age.

Thang you very much...Ahuh!

But... did Elvis really die on 16 August 1977? There are plenty of people who think not.

Some Elvis fans think that The King, as he was known, did not die at all. Instead, sick of his current existence, the theory goes that he went into hiding and created a new life for himself. Various claims have been made (not all of them 100% serious):

★ **Elvis regularly makes prank phone calls. His favourite is apparently to ask people, 'Is your refrigerator running?' When they say yes, he asks, 'How, without any legs?'**

★ **Elvis is regularly seen shopping at K-mart stores.**

★ **Elvis is sometimes claimed to have retrained as a doctor, and spent his time delivering babies.**

## ★ The truth is...

Elvis would be in his late 70s if he were alive today, so — unlike Hitler — it wouldn't be impossible for him to still be around. BUT, there's no real doubt that he did die in 1977. Elvis was known to have serious health problems, and his family, doctors, friends and managers all saw the body, which was also secretly photographed.

Verdict : ____ **FICTION** ____

# When animals ATTACK!

## Escaping killer bees

Killer bees are just like ordinary bees — except much more aggressive. When disturbed, they will pour out of their hive and chase away their target. If you meet these buzzing terrors...

### DO

Run like crazy – the bees sometimes chase their victims for hundreds of metres before giving up.

Wrap something around your face to stop your eyes being stung (but make sure you can still see where you're going!)

### Don't

Dive into water – the bees will just wait for you to surface.

Wave your hands and arms – bees are attracted to movement.

# Vultures attack live victims

## Imagine the scene...

You're lost in the desert (perhaps your sand-boarding expedition has gone back to the hotel without you). You've been out there in the heat for a long time, and your strength is failing. Then you see something you've been dreading: vultures, circling!!

You sit to rest in the shade of a rock, and a vulture lands nearby. Its bare neck and head look evil. You know vultures are featherless so that the birds can more easily stick their heads inside dead creatures. Another vulture lands, and another. They start to hop closer, then to peck at your feet.

Are you about to be become lunch for a wake* of vultures — while you're still alive?

## The truth is...

It could happen, though you'd have to be very weak — too weak to move, probably. Vultures prefer their food to be dead, but they do occasionally attack dying prey.

*'Wake' is the word for a group of feeding vultures. Circling vultures are often called a 'kettle'. A group in a tree is called a 'committee', 'venue' or 'volt'.

Verdict : _____

# The Wild West was dangerous, violent and very, very wild

In Westerns, that's certainly how it looks — they tell the story of life in the Western USA in the late 19th century. The cowboys in these movies spent most of their time involved in gunfights and saloon shoot-outs. They galloped across prairies, Stetsons pulled low, rifles at the ready. And they were pretty good at sliding drinks along bars without spilling them, too. Sometimes, they even looked after cows. Meanwhile, outlaws wreaked havoc and sheriffs tried to keep the peace. Life was never dull, often dangerous and always exciting.

**And the truth is...**

Before the moviemakers became involved, American frontier families headed out west and life was very hard. Cowboys looked after cows, because that was their job. It's doubtful whether many of them lived lives as daring and glamorous as in the Westerns — these were mostly stories dreamed up by Hollywood. In fact, the most common cause of death for cowboys was not gunfights, but horse-riding accidents.

Gunfights did happen, but they were rare. The Gunfight at the OK Corral was one event that really did take place. It only lasted 30 seconds, but that was long enough to kill three outlaws, wound three other men and give Wyatt Earp the reputation as being the toughest and deadliest gunman of the Old West. But the truth is, he probably didn't have that much competition.

Verdict : **FICTION**

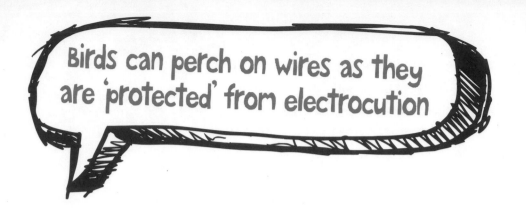

## Birds can perch on wires as they are 'protected' from electrocution

We all know that electricity cables are dangerous. You don't go messing around near electricity pylons — touch one of those wires and you might not live to tell anyone about how stupid you've been. So how come birds can stand on the wires and not suffer any ill-effects? It must be because birds have some kind of insulation on their feet that protects them from the electric current. Or is it something else?

## And the truth is...

The answer lies in how electricity travels. Electricity needs a start and end point and something to travel on from one to the other. This is called a circuit. Electricity also likes to take the easiest path, which is important for the birds, as is the fact that some substances conduct electricity better than other materials. When birds sit on a wire the electricity continues on its path, because the wire conducts electricity better than birds do. However if the bird had one foot on the wire and one on something else — like the pole for example — then the bird would make a new circuit, the electricity would flow through the bird and the bird would get frazzled.

Verdict : **FICTION**

## A man once flew 5 km upward in a garden chair

Many people dream of having their own personal flying device. Few of us ever decide to make one out of a garden chair and some balloons — and then take it on a 5-km-high test flight. But that's just what happened one day in Los Angeles, USA.

Larry Walters bought himself 45 weather balloons and a bottle of helium gas. He tied the balloons tightly to a garden chair, and tied the chair to his pickup truck. Next Larry filled the balloons with helium, which caused the chair to lift off. Larry climbed aboard and strapped himself to the chair. He took along an air pistol, to shoot some of the balloons when he was ready to descend.

Larry released the rope from the pickup, and took off.

After floating around at the same height as international jet flights (he was spotted by at least one surprised pilot), Larry began to get cold. So he shot out some of his balloons... and floated back down to Earth. Phew-ey.

## ★ And the truth is...

This all really happened, on 2 July 1982.

Verdict : _____ incredible, but it's a...

# Cheese gives you nightmares

In the Charles Dickens story *A Christmas Carol*, the miser Scrooge is visited in the night by disturbing visions. He blames the visions on bad dreams, caused by eating, 'a crumb of cheese' just before going to bed.

Scrooge is not alone. Many people think that eating cheese too close to bedtime will give them nightmares. But is this long-standing urban myth actually true?

## ⭐ The fact is...

An investigation in 2005 discovered that there is a connection between cheese and dreams.
People were given a small piece of cheese to eat before bed, then asked to record their dreams. Three-quarters of them said they slept well, and most remembered their dreams more clearly than usual. People who ate blue cheese had especially vivid dreams.

No one, though, reported that their dreams were nightmares.

Verdict :

## Chocolate is poisonous to dogs

This is a myth that doesn't really seem to make sense. After all, dogs are very like humans — that's why animal-testing laboratories test products on dogs before approving them for human consumption. If *we* can eat chocolate, surely dogs must be able to as well? Especially as they seem to like it so much...

## ★ The truth is...

Chocolate contains a chemical called theobromine, which in dogs causes muscle tremors, seizures or even heart attacks.
So it is poisonous to dogs, who don't have to eat very much of it to get sick or die.

Verdict : _____

Other things (truly) poisonous to dogs:

It's not only chocolate! You also need to make sure dogs don't snaffle down:

1. Grapes and raisins

2. Onions

3. Macadamia nuts

## Piranha fish can strip a body of its flesh in seconds

Never — NEVER! — go swimming in a South American river if you have an open wound. Within seconds schools of bloodthirsty piranhas will gather round your body. Their tiny teeth will rip away little chunks of flesh, and in the blink of an eye, you will have been stripped to the bone. All that's left will be a skeleton, sinking to the bottom of the river.

At least, that's what one of the most common animal myths tells you. But would a school of piranha *really* strip a human of flesh in seconds?

### ★ The truth is...

Piranha fish do have sharp little teeth, and can give a nasty bite. But they rarely attack humans, and then only usually by accident. The myth grew up when US President Teddy Roosevelt witnessed a publicity stunt in which starved piranhas stripped a cow to the bone. Roosevelt later wrote that, 'blood in the water excites them to madness'.

Verdict : _____ **FICTION** _____

## All pirates were men

Pirates ruled the seas in the 18th century. They swashbuckled and swore. They spoke in deep, booming voices, terrifying the poor souls whose galleons they were plundering. So they must all have been men, because this was *hardly* ladylike behaviour.

# ⭐ And the truth is...

Step aside, **Blackbeard**. Women were just as good as men at being pirates.

**Jeanne de Clisson** was known as the Lioness of Brittany. She lurked in the English Channel, laying in wait for warships. But she never killed everyone on board — she always left two or three sailors alive so they could tell everyone back at home who had attacked them.

**Grace O'Malley** was an Irish pirate who was known as the Sea Queen of Connaught. Her exploits — including theft, abduction and murder — are legendary.

Then there was **Mary Read**, whose ship was taken over by pirates in the early 18th century. She became one of them, sailing the Caribbean with another female pirate, **Anne Bonny** and Calico Jack, who was all for equality on the high seas.

Verdict : **FICTION**

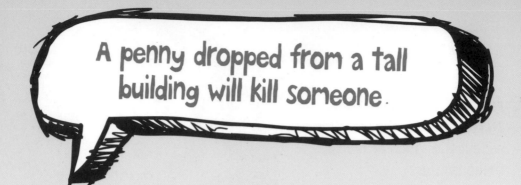

## A penny dropped from a tall building will kill someone.

There are various versions of this story, involving the Empire State Building or the Eiffel Tower, but the general theme is the same — if you drop a small coin from a very tall building you could kill someone. The idea is that a coin falling from a great height will pick up so much speed it will be travelling as fast as a bullet. So don't drop coins out of a high window or you could be up on a murder charge.

### ★ And the truth is...

Objects don't keep speeding up as they fall, instead they reach 'terminal velocity', the fastest speed gravity will pull them to Earth. A penny's terminal velocity is about 2.4m/sec (8.8 ft/ sec), BUT — and as you can see it's a big but — pennies do not fly through the air well. Their shape is not aerodynamic, so they flutter and spin through the air which slows them down. Also the air around big buildings is gusty which would slow the penny down further.

By the time the penny reaches the ground, the worst it is likely to do is give somebody a bruise.

Verdict :— **FICTION**

# A few surprising sleep facts

 Top-notch scientist Einstein liked to give his brain plenty of rest. He used to sleep for 12 hours every day.

 Former British prime minister Margaret Thatcher was famous for needing only 4 hours sleep each night – though she also used to take a nap during the day. Another prime minister, Winston Churchill, got into bed for a sleep every afternoon.

 Elizabethans who couldn't sleep used to rub dormouse fat on the soles of their feet (NB this wouldn't work).

 Counting imaginary sheep is a rubbish way of trying to get to sleep (though possibly not as rubbish as rubbing dormouse fat on your feet). Imagining a relaxing scene is a much better technique.

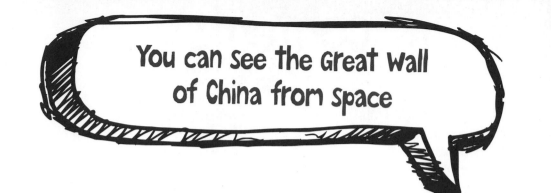

# You can See the Great Wall of China from Space

For years, people have believed that it's possible to see the Great Wall of China from space, using only the naked eye. The myth actually appears in school books and board games around the world. In fact, some people will even tell you that the Great Wall is the only artificial structure that can be seen from space. But is it true?

## ★ The fact is...

In 2003, Yang Liwei became the first Chinese person to visit space, in the spacecraft Shenzhou V. He looked pretty hard for the Great Wall — but when he returned to Earth, Yang had to admit that he hadn't been able to see it, even though he'd flown above it. The Chinese government immediately began to remove the claim from school textbooks.

Verdict : ——  ——

# contents

## Animals

# History

# Science

# urban Myths

*Truth or Busted: The Fact or Fiction Behind Science*
first published in 2012 by Wayland
*Truth or Busted: The Fact or Fiction Behind History*
first published in 2012 by Wayland
*Truth or Busted: The Fact or Fiction Behind Animals*
first published in 2012 by Wayland
*Truth or Busted: The Fact or Fiction Behind Urban Myths*
first published in 2014 by Wayland

Authors: Kay Barnham (History),
Paul Harrison (Science),
Paul Mason (Animals and Urban Myths)
Illustrations : Alan Irvine, Shutterstock

This editon published in 2016 by Wayland
© 2016, Wayland

Carmelite House, 50 Victoria Embankment, London EC4Y 0DZ
Wayland is an imprint of Hachette Children's Group

First published in French in 2014 by Hachette Livre
© 2014, Hachette Livre/Deux Coqs d'Or.
43 quai de Grenelle - 75015 Paris

Printed in China